Foreword

Executive summary

Introduction

Visit reports

Perspectives

Foreword

E-learning, flexible learning, online delivery, virtual learning environments, fifth generation of distance education, e-business, staff involvement, diversifying student groups, copyright. These are only a few of the more frequent keywords one will come across when reading or glancing through this book: the result of 16 experiences and a considerable number of lessons learned from a two-week study visit to Australian higher education institutions during March 2002.

Preparations began in Spring 2001. At that time, SURF Education, part of the SURF Foundation in the Netherlands, started to formally extend their international partnerships with, among others, the Association for Learning and Technology (ALT) in the UK. After having met on several occasions, including the ALT conferences and the European Academic Software Awards, SURF Education invited 'kindred spirit' ALT to intensify their international relationship. Having both a profound basis within the higher education field and a transparent innovation policy, they are now jointly organising reciprocal study visits and international conferences. One of their first events was the 'IT in Higher Education' experience in Australia during March 2002.

Many of our Australian colleagues contributed directly or indirectly to a successful study trip. We especially want to thank Gerry Lefoe (University of Wollongong) for being such a good guide in our search for interesting places to visit and for hosting us at the University of Wollongong.

Furthermore, we want to thank our other Australian hosts: Simon Housego (University of Technology Sydney), John Messing (Charles Sturt University), Ron Oliver (Edith Cowan University), Rob Philips (Murdoch University), Meg O'Reilly (Southern Cross University),

Helmut Geiblinger (Queensland University of Technology), Jan Dook (University of Western Australia), Stuart Young (West One), Lynda Davies (Griffith University), Susan Brosnan (University of Southern Queensland), Christine Mason (University of Melbourne), Anthony Gilding (Monash University), Rod Sims (Deakin University), John Findlay (Zing Conference Systems), and Jeremy Stuparich, Judd Murray and Michael Galagher (Department for Education, Science and Training).

As the co-ordinator and organiser of the trip, I personally want to thank all my Dutch, Belgium and UK colleagues for a very intensive, but enjoyable time; both in and outside Australia! I especially want to thank Bas Cordewener and Tom Dousma from SURF Education for making the trip happen and Rhonda Riachi (ALT) for her advice and efforts in helping me organise and co-ordinate the experience. I would also like to thank the LTSN Generic Centre for enabling the results to be published in this book.

In conclusion, this study trip was, for many of us, the first time in Australia, so the potential for gaining information and experiencing cultural overload was quite high. However, the ravages of barbecues, beaches and Chardonnay did not stop us from bringing back impressions of the different approaches to ICT in Australia. We were warmly welcomed at all institutions and, on the whole, our hosts were quite frank about the advantages as well as the disadvantages of the approaches they had taken to ICT implementation.

We send our heartfelt thanks to everyone in Australia who helped make it such a success.

Petra Boezerooy
CHEPS Universiteit Twente

Executive summary

This chapter summarises the major findings and conclusions of a two-week study visit to Australia during March 2002. This trip was a joint initiative of the SURF Foundation in the Netherlands and the Association for Learning Technology (ALT) in the UK.

The general context of Australian higher education

- Change in Federal Government policy, comprising a requirement that the higher education sector teach more students and improve 'quality' while keeping funding the same or at reduced levels, with a further expectation that students should contribute more to the cost of their higher and further education.

- Higher education institutions are preparing for the new model of quality assurance, which was unveiled in Australia in March 2002.

- Whereas the UK and the Netherlands have dedicated Open Universities, many Australian universities have a high commitment to distance learning, which is often based in the historical development of their institution. Distance learning in Australia often uses traditional modes of delivery and includes little e-learning. Other universities have decided to concentrate on on campus education and offer very little distance learning. However, the distinction between on campus and distance students is becoming blurred as more students are living locally but taking 'distance' modules.

- Universities have different strategies leading to a differentiation in profile. Profiles range from universities focusing on serving the region to universities that opt for a global market.

Emphasis on flexibility instead of online or e-Learning

The term flexibility is often used within Australian higher education institutions, although it is not easily defined and it should not be mistaken as a synonym for online and/or distance education. In order to survive and thrive, Australian universities in the 21st century need to offer their learners more choice across many aspects of their learning experience. Universities, faculties and individual staff must make pragmatic choices about the ingredients they choose for their own particular 'flexibility recipe' (flexibility choices in administration, pedagogy and delivery).

Consolidation and institutionalisation

From initiation, to implementation towards institutionalisation – these phases can all be seen in Australian higher education. The general trend is that most institutions visited move from the implementation towards the institutionalisation phase, as ICT developments in many of the institutions visited are no longer only at the experimental level, but very often integrated into the mainstream operations of the particular institution. This leads to a focused, pragmatic use of ICT to bring about consolidation and economies of scale.

University-wide implementation

The need to professionally support and maintain a dispersed student body is leading to innovative technology systems for support and administration. In some institutions one can see the integration of these support and administrative processes with the teaching and learning systems (portals). In these settings libraries, IT-centres and teaching & learning centres are collaborating to cover all necessary tasks. There is a focus on the development of university-wide knowledge/data object management systems to provide security (intellectual property and data protection), consistency, and economies (in that data/knowledge will not be needlessly duplicated). In many setting autonomy of the instructors and faculties is an issue when implementing, for example, Virtual Learning Environments (VLE). Instructors on courses with students at a distance are more easily convinced of the advantages of VLEs compared to instructors on campus-based courses.

Technology: Virtual Learning Environments and portals

Most Australian universities have selected a Virtual Learning Environment (VLE) for their learning and teaching. This VLE may be part of a managed learning environment (MLE) and/or linked to their university portal. The majority have chosen a commercial VLE, with Blackboard and WebCT sharing the market. Some universities have developed their own in-house system. The table below refers to the universities visited and gives details of the software, extent of use and URL of the University portal or VLE. Most of these portals and VLEs have been given names which relate to, and identify, the institution. This personalises the portal/LE for the user and makes them feel part of the institution.

University	Name	Software	URL
Charles Sturt (CSU)	myCSU	Own Considering Blackboard	my.csu.edu.au
Deakin	Deakin Online	Currently, FirstClass and Topclass Choosing between BB and WebCT	www.deakin.edu.au/deakinonline
Edith Cowan (ECU)	MyECU	Blackboard	http://MyECU.ecu.edu.au
Griffith–Logan	Learning@GU	Blackboard	www2.gu.edu.au/
Melbourne		Moving to WebCT	http://webraft.its.unimelb.edu.au/
Monash		WebCT and own	https://my.monash.edu.au/
Murdoch	Murdoch Online	WebCT	www.murdoch.edu.au/online/
Queensland University of Technology (QUT)	QUTVirtual OLT	Variety of tools	https://qutvirtual.qut.edu.au/ https://olt.qut.edu.au/
Southern Cross (SCU)	MySCU	Blackboard	http://study.scu.edu.au
University Southern Queensland (USQ)	USQOnline	NextEd (with Blackboard) and WebCT	www.usqonline.com.au/
University Technology Sydney (UTS)		Blackboard	http://online.uts.edu.au/
University Western Australia (UWA)		WebCT	
West One		WebCT	
Wollongong		WebCT	www.uow.edu.au/LOL/

Table 1: Virtual learning environments & portals in Australia

At some universities, like Southern Cross, QUT and Murdoch, a campus-wide VLE has been implemented, while at others the implementation of the VLEs is still mainly at the pilot stage within faculties and is not yet campus-wide. The key issues concerning the implementation are academic ownership, the development of the content, staff support and development within a changing culture. There has been little evaluation of the effect of VLEs on student learning.

Teaching and learning

The major pedagogies underlying e-learning in Australia are flexible learning and constructivism. Problem-based learning is used extensively in medicine, for example, at Monash and Melbourne. The motives behind using these pedagogies are a desire to increase the quality of learning and teaching and commercial perspectives. Although there is some attention for the pedagogies underlying e-learning, very often technology implementation or implementations of e-learning strategies primarily appear to be made with regard to increasing flexibility of delivery, rather than to any commitment to improve teaching and learning from a pedagogical basis.

Student population

The growth in diversity of the student population and the increase in numbers are encouraging universities to consider new patterns of learning and teaching. These are aimed at increasing greater flexibility of access from locations other than the traditional campus, for example, from home and from the workplace. This greater diversity of student background is also resulting in the need to make changes to student support and guidance structures and processes. Students enter university with less well-developed study habits, needing a wider range of study and language support.

Research and the teaching and learning centres

Australia has an international reputation for research into learning technologies. Such work does not appear to be the direct driver for the increased use of these technologies though it significantly contributes to their successful use and in some cases will have led implementation. In many of the Australian teaching and learning centres research into learning technologies is an important task. In some of the universities these teaching and learning units play a leading role in the implementation of their university's strategy in partnership with support from central administration. The units flourish in structures that take campus-wide use of new technologies seriously and encourage a high profile. In some other cases the technology is seen more as a means, and reflective research on how it is used has a low profile.

Libraries and information services

The university library and information services visited utilised technological developments to increase accessibility to, and availability of, library products and services. Deakin University, Charles Sturt University, Southern Cross University and University Southern Queensland saw ICT as a means of maintaining equity of opportunity and service to both on and off campus users. Electronic desktop delivery of required items is becoming a standard service, with electronic signatures fulfilling copyright requirements for a signed declaration form.

Services range from supporting traditional information sources (Deakin University posts books around the world and pays for students to return them), to investigating digital printing on demand (Deakin University and Southern Cross University).

The difficulties of providing an adequate reference service to students based all round the world and, or wishing to work 24/7 have been solved in a number of ways. University of Technology Sydney has formed a reciprocal arrangement with a Scottish University to provide a real-time 'ask a question live' service.

Copyright

In early 2001, the Australian Government passed the Copyright Amendment (Digital Agenda) Act. This has implications in terms of both how libraries can supply information (for example, desktop electronic delivery), but also the need to keep accurate up-to-date records to satisfy the requirements of the Act. At University of Technology Sydney for example, the library has the controlling authority for all the institution's copyright matters. Deakin University is investigating a digital object management system, partly to maximise use of materials and to cut down on duplication, but also to keep track of copyright requests.

Innovation

There are many innovative projects being undertaken at Australian universities. The following table summarises case studies of innovations that are described in detail in the other chapters.

Project title	University	Brief description
	Melbourne	Showcase examples www.infodiv.unimelb.edu.au/telars/cds/services/gdprojshowcase.shtml
Digital Object Management Systems (DOMS)	Deakin	Aim to tag DOMS so that the university knows what is available, where it is and how it is being used.
Digital portfolio	Edith Cowan	The development of a digital portfolio system to be used by students for reflection and study planning.
Flexible Pedagogies Initiative		Exploring and developing aspects of flexibility http://education.qut.edu.au/fo/fpi/fpihomebase.html
ILectures	University of Western Australia	Audio recordings with PowerPoint slides of 150 lectures a week available within 3 hours of the lecture (http://ilectures.uwa.edu.au)
South coast arts	Wollongong	Development of provision to outreach centres
USQAssist	University of Southern Queensland	The automated project builds on previous knowledge creating an increasingly populating database of answers to queries

Table 2: Examples of innovation projects

Partnerships

Many of the Australian higher education institutions do have various forms of partnerships (e.g. with both national and international educational institutions and with the industry). One of the main motives for seeking such partnerships is the fact that Australian universities need external funding sources to meet their budgets. The role of ICT in the partnerships is an on-going point of attention. Technology, particularly Web-based resources and systems, are indispensable for the partnerships. Furthermore, internationalisation is of growing strategic importance to the university sector as the income from fee-paying students is an important and growing source of university revenue. Overseas fee-paying students contribute 79% of the fee-paying revenue. The use of technology is essential for the ambitions of Australian universities with respect to increasing numbers of off-shore and off campus students.

Conclusion

The overall impressions from the institutions visited were positive; all universities were taking technology seriously and were working hard to develop the teams of staff necessary to move towards more flexible provision of courses. Staff development was regarded as essential to the successful implementation of technology. In many respects it appeared that the institutions visited were at the same stage as those in the UK and the Netherlands. The pedagogical and technical challenges posed by the roll-out of virtual learning environments (e.g. WebCT and Blackboard) courses was familiar territory for UK and Dutch colleagues. In some respects it appeared that the institutions visited were ahead of many of the UK and Dutch universities. The support systems (teaching and learning centres) are more mature and developed, technology is seen as essential for the ambitions of Australian universities with respect to increasing numbers of off-shore and off campus students, and the need to professionally support and maintain a dispersed student body are leading to innovative technology systems for support and administration. With a great diversity in profile, Australian universities have an outspoken strategy, in which the role of ICT is identified.

Introduction

Background

The study visit to Australia was a joint initiative of the SURF[1] Foundation in the Netherlands and the Association for Learning Technology (ALT[2]) in the UK. Sixteen members of ALT and SURF visited 13 universities (see the institutions marked * in Table 3) and the vocationally oriented agency, 'West One', during two weeks in March 2002, to compare ICT developments between the Netherlands, UK and Australia. Small groups were formed to visit each institution (no more than six persons) and informal meetings were held with a wide range of staff involved in policy development and practice of ICT in the institutions. For each institution, visit reports have been written, incorporating specific themes (known as 'perspectives') to focus the visits: e-learning in Australia, strategic implementation and partnerships/relationships. Both the visit reports and the perspectives are part of this book[3]. More general information about e-learning in Australia can be found in this chapter.

Higher Education in Australia

There are 38 publicly funded universities in Australia and another seven higher education institutions or colleges which receive public funds. In 2001 these institutions served over 600,000 internal students and over 102,000 external students (DETYA, 2002). There are significant differences between Australian universities that reflect the institution's age, reputation, location, composition of the student cohort, curriculum content, research profile and funding sources. Marginson grouped the various Australian higher education institutions together

on the basis of age (Marginson and Considine, 2000). Marginson identifies 5 types of institutions:

1. The Sandstone universities, the oldest foundations in each state, founded pre-World War One. They tend to be research intensive institutions. All have some sandstone buildings.

2. The Redbricks, founded in the 1940s-1950s, the strongest of the post-second world war universities. Commonly research intensive institutions. Redbrick is more than evident in their architecture.

3. The Gumtrees, universities founded later in the post-war period, between 1960 and 1975. Many of the sites of these universities were planted with native trees (hence 'Gumtrees'). Often located in regional or outer-suburban locations.

4. The Unitechs, largest of the old Colleges of Advanced Education (CAE) in five states, with a strong vocational and industry orientation. The architecture in this group ranges from early Fordism/Taylorism, to utilitarian modern.

5. The New Universities, a heterogeneous group of post-1986 foundations. In their buildings utilitarian recency combines with secondary school leftovers from the CAE Education period.

e-Learning in Australia

Michael Galagher[4]

When discussing the term 'e-learning', we will be referring to the use of digital technologies to support and deliver some or all of the teaching

1 www.surf.nl
2 www.alt.ac.uk
3 Both the visit reports and the perspectives are reflections of the ICT developments of the higher education institutions visited during March 2002. Meanwhile, many of these institutions have continued to move on from the point where they were at the time of our visit.
4 Michael Galagher is First Assistant Secretary of the Higher Education Division of the Australian Department of Education, Training and Youth Affairs. We were very pleased that some parts of his paper, written for the 7th OECD/Japan seminar on 'E-learning in Post-Secondary Education: Trends, Issues and Policy Changes Ahead' 5-6 June 2001, could be included in this introduction.

and learning for a particular unit of study. Primarily this is the use of the communications power of the Internet to deliver an interactive learning environment to students without constraints of time or geography. It is important, though, not to confuse the very important developments in technology that help to deliver education with the value of the education itself. Education has always been delivered to students by a variety of methods and students have always employed a variety of modes of learning, including informal modes such as discussing subject materials with other students, friends or family (Masie, 2001).

The environment for e-Learning

E-learning in Australia has developed from a very long history of post-secondary distance education, with the first print-based distance education program offered to university students in 1911 (Department of Employment, Education and Training, 1993). Distance education options were initially offered by universities because of the need to overcome the often very large distances that separated students from a higher education institution. Australia is a very large landmass – over 7.6 million square kilometres – with a relatively small population of just over 19 million (Australian Bureau of Statistics, 2001a). While these long distances still remain

Sandstones	Redbricks	Gumtrees	Unitechs	New Universities
Sydney	Monash*	Griffith*	University Technology Sydney*	Edith Cowan*
Queensland*	University of New South Wales	Newcastle	Queenslands University of Technology*	Central Qld
Western Australia*	Australian National University	Flinders	Royal Melbourne Institute of Technology	Southern Cross*
Adelaide		James Cook	Curtin	Western Sydney
Tasmania		Deakin*	Sth. Aust.	Charles Sturt*
Melbourne*		La Trobe		Victoria University of Technology
		Macquarie		Southern Qld
		Wollongong*		Canberra
		Murdoch *		Australian Catholic University
		New England		Northern Territory
				Swinburne
				Ballarat
				Sunshine Coast

Table 3 shows the overview of all publicly funded Australian higher education institutions, based on Marginson's taxonomy of Australian universities. During the two-weeks study trip, we visited 13 of these institutions (marked *) as well as West One, an agency, set up by the State of Western Australia, whose role is to 'support the Western Australian vocational sector in utilising technology for learning and managing associated change'.

for many students, the overall nature of the demand for distance education has changed in recent years, with significant numbers of city-based students choosing distance education for the convenience of not having to visit a university campus (Cumpston et al, 2001). This reflects another important factor – the highly urbanised nature of Australia with over 60% of people living in the eight capital cities, and that number is projected to grow in the coming years (Australian Bureau of Statistics, 1999). Also interesting are reports of the increasing number of on campus students making use of distance education and e-learning materials, despite not being located remotely from a university.

Demand for e-Learning

The move to e-learning has been assisted on the demand side by high access levels to computers and the Internet, with 66% of Australian adults having used a computer and 50% of adults having accessed the Internet in the twelve months to November 2000 (Australian Bureau of Statistics, 2001b). A private research firm claims that by February 2001 67% of Australian Internet users had used the Internet regularly for about two years and that 83% used the Internet in the week prior to the survey (Red Sheriff, 2001; Centeno, 2001). University student access levels to technology appear to be even higher than for the general population, with a recent survey of tertiary students in Australia finding that over 95% of university students reported making regular use of information and communications technology (ICT) (Oliver and Towers, 2000).

As well as an increase in access to, and use of, ICT, there has also been a corresponding and perhaps causal change in the profile of students engaging in education in university. Between 1994 and 1999 there was a 9% increase in the proportion of students who were studying full time, yet who were also in paid employment (McInnes, 2000). This change is also noted in the United States and other parts of the developed world in the form of what a study by Cunningham et al (2000) called the 'learner-earner' – the full time student who also has a paid job. Cunningham also identifies growth in numbers of the 'earner-learner' – the person with a full-time job who undertakes study. These developments in the student profile mean that students trying to juggle both work and study are naturally interested in increased flexibility – such as reducing or eliminating the number of hours they have to spend on campus – and the ability to fast-track their education. These are all factors leading to further demand for flexible forms of education such as e-learning.

Supply of e-Learning

Most Australian universities offer some form of distance or flexible education involving e-learning, with those universities at the leading edge offering fully online courses, leading to awards ranging from certificates to masters degrees in disciplines as diverse as nursing and accounting.

What is known as distance, external or flexible education has moved through a number of generations since the first correspondence students, and the development of these modes of education has taken advantage of new technologies as they came to hand. To explain these changes over time, Taylor (2001) identifies five generations of distance education in his model of the development of this teaching mode, the last two of which can be described as levels of e-learning. The levels are:

- The correspondence model, where learning materials are print-based;

- The multimedia model, where there is a variety of ways of presenting the learning materials, whether by print, audiotape, video tape or computer-based learning;

- The telelearning model, in which modes of presentation of learning material include audio or video-conferencing and broadcast TV or radio;

- The flexible learning model, where students have access to interactive multimedia online, computer mediated communication and Internet-based resources; and,

- The intelligent flexible learning model, which builds on the fourth generation but will also allow 'campus portal access to institutional processes and resources', allowing the institution to reduce its variable costs to close to zero.

An increasing number of Australian universities are offering access to education by e-learning and are moving to exploit the fifth generation model. These include education offered directly through universities with longstanding experience and expertise in distance education, such as Charles Sturt University, Deakin University and the University of Southern Queensland (all three visited during the study trip, see for more information the visit reports of these institutions).

While many universities are restructuring to be able to offer more e-learning options for students, there is an argument that these changes are largely supply driven by universities that wish to exploit the opportunities offered by the new technology, and are not the result of demand by most Australian students. The demand is largely restricted to the earner-learners who need to continue their studies while working full time (Ryan, 2001). Indeed the targets of this university supply-driven market are students outside the relatively small Australian market and the earner learners, who may be supported by their employers or are confident that their investment in learning will assist their careers and their earning future. Although historically Australian students have not been used to paying directly for their education and so have been reluctant to pay the extra cost of e-learning, many can afford to pay the often substantial fees charged for e-learning units (Whyte, 2001).

Student numbers involved in e-Learning

In 2001, 14% (102,000) of all students studying at Australian universities, both domestic and overseas students, were studying by what is described in statistics as 'external' education. The definition of 'external' in the statistics collected by the Department of Education, Training and Youth Affairs is fairly broad and includes 'all units of study for which the student is enrolled involv[ing] special arrangements whereby lesson materials, assignments etc. are delivered to the student, and any associated attendance at the institution is of an incidental, special or voluntary nature' (Department of Education, Training and Youth Affairs, 2002).

The external category therefore includes most students undertaking e-learning as well as distance education by paper-based and mixed mode study, so it is difficult to determine the exact number of students involved in e-learning with Australian higher education institutions. Furthermore, the overall picture of the number of students involved in e-learning is clouded by the fact that significant numbers of on campus students choose to study some subjects or aspects of their course online.

Australia's leading universities in the field of distance education and e-learning boast very high numbers of external students, with three of Australia's universities having approximately 65-75% of their students studying off campus. As many of these students are studying part time, this slightly overstates the full impact of the numbers, but they are certainly significant.

Statistics on courses and units of study taught by e-Learning[5]

In order to ascertain the current extent of online education in Australian universities, the Department of Education, Science and Training (DEST) commissioned a study. Data were collected from 40 out of the 43 universities in Australia between August and December 2001. Before the main findings of the survey into online courses, units and services as at December 2001 are presented, first of all definitions of online delivery in Australian higher education are described.

The Department of Education, Science and Training (DEST), in consultation with experts drawn from the higher education sector, developed its own working definitions of online delivery, based on the degree of dependence on the web for delivery. The DEST survey defined the online delivery under three major categories:

Mode A – web supplemented

In this category, participation online is optional for the student. Enrolled students can access information on units of study that is additional to that available in the university's calendar or handbook. The information may include course descriptions and study guides, examination information, assessment overview, reading lists and other online learning resources. The information is used to supplement traditional forms of delivery.

Mode B – web dependent

Participation online for each activity in the following three categories is a compulsory requirement of participation, although some traditional on campus component is retained:

- Students need to use the web to interact with the education content necessary for study; or,

- It is a compulsory requirement of study that students must use the web to communicate with staff and/or other students; or,

- Students need to use the web both to interact with content and to communicate with staff and/or other students.

Mode C – fully online

There is no on campus direct contact component in this mode. All interactions with staff and students, education content, learning activities, assessment and support services are integrated and delivered online.

The main findings of the survey, commissioned by DEST, are described below:

Online courses: key findings

- The survey found that there were 207 fully online courses offered by 23 Australian universities. Sixty-five of these courses (31%) are delivered only by online mode.

- The majority (90%) of online courses are at postgraduate level. In general, postgraduate online courses show a tendency towards specialised courses rather than generalist qualifications.

15

5 www.dest.gov.au/highered/occpaper/02a/default.htm Universities online: a survey of online education and services in Australia, Higher Education Group, Department of Education, Science and Training, March 2002

- Over a quarter of online courses are in the field of Management and Commerce (55 courses). Education represents a further 35 courses and Health 32 courses. The remaining 85 courses are spread across:
  1) Natural and Physical Sciences;
  2) Information Technology;
  3) Engineering and Related Technologies;
  4) Agriculture, Environmental and Related Studies;
  5) Society and Culture;
  6) Creative Arts;
  7) Mixed Programs.

- There is little duplication reported of online courses offered. The only duplication of courses is as follows: five universities offer online Graduate Diplomas in e-Commerce or e-Business and four universities offer online Graduate Certificates in Online Learning or Flexible Learning.

Online units and web-supplemented units: key findings

- The use of the Internet in university units ranges from a high of 99 or 100% of units in seven universities to a low of 9% in one university. All universities are employing the Web to some extent for teaching and learning purposes.

- Universities reported that 50,704 of their units (54%) have content available on the Web.

- The most prevalent form of online delivery was Web-supplemented with 46% of units. Fully online units represent a small percentage of units, i.e. 1.4%, (0.8% of undergraduate units, 2.7% of postgraduate units).

- The discipline areas that have the highest percentage of fully online units are: Management and Commerce with 2.6% fully online units, Education 2.5%, Information Technology 2.3% and Health 2.2%.

- The discipline areas that make least use of the Web are Food, Hospitality and Personal Services (56.6% make no use of the Web), Creative Arts (55.7%), and Society and Culture (52.1%).

- Information and Technology (I.T.) units appear to make the highest use of the Web, compared with other discipline areas; 40.5% of I.T. units are either fully online or Web-dependent.

Online services: key findings

- Most universities (87.5%) provide an Intranet, which can be accessed by all students, with 70% providing access to the Intranet from off campus.

- A high percentage of universities (92.5%) have made their university handbook and/or calendar available online.

- Online access to university libraries is high. Ninety-five% of universities provide access to their university library catalogue via the Internet, 90% provide access to online journals and monographs and 82.5% provide online reservation of books.

- Universities use a number of commercial and in-house courseware management systems, sometimes several systems within the same institution, the most frequently used of which are: WebCT (29 universities), in-house systems (20 universities) and Blackboard (17 universities).

- Online registration and enrolment services are not widespread. 40% of universities offer online registration or enrolment for existing students; only 27.5% offer this service for new students and 30% provide online variation of enrolment.

- Online payment of fees is also not yet widely available, with only 30% of universities offering this facility to all students.

- Online learning support for students is available in 57% of universities and 45% provide online training in ICT skills.

Regulations and quality assurance mechanisms

Australian regulations and quality assurance mechanisms in higher education have never distinguished between the methods of teaching and learning employed, whether they be the more traditional on campus face-to-face learning, or whether they be by paper-based distance education, e-learning or another teaching and learning method. The focus has always been on the quality of the pedagogical approach and on the use of whatever technology allows the student and teacher the best flexibility and outcome.

E-learning, flexible learning, distance education, external education and education by correspondence are all varieties of the same thing – they all involve the ongoing efforts of university teachers to develop the appropriate pedagogy and to use the best and most effective of the available technologies to deliver education to students. Regulations and quality assurance mechanisms for e-learning are therefore the same as the broad regulatory regime that applies to universities and other higher education institutions in Australia with regard to other forms of teaching and learning.

Bibliography

Australian Bureau of Statistics, 1999. Australian Social Trends 1999. Australian Bureau of Statistics, Canberra. Catalogue number 4102.0

Australian Bureau of Statistics, 2001a. Australia Now: A Statistical Profile. **www.abs.gov.au/ausstats/abs@.nsf/ w2.6.1?OpenView**

Australian Bureau of Statistics, 2001b. Use of the Internet by Householders, Australia. Australian Bureau of Statistics, Canberra. Catalogue number 8147.0

Centeno, C. 2001. Aussie Internet usage advances, eStatNews, eMarketer, 9 May. **www.emarketer.com/estatnews/estats/easia /20010509_red_aussie.html?ref=wn**

Cumpston, A et al. 2001. Atlas of higher education: a community focus. Occasional Paper Series, Department of Education, Training and Youth Affairs. **www.detya.gov.au/uniatlas**

Cunningham, S et al. 2000. The Business of Borderless Education. Evaluations and Investigations Programme, Higher Education Division, Department of Education, Training and Youth Affairs. **www.detya.gov.au/archive/highered/ eippubs/eip00_3/execsum.htm**

Department of Employment, Education and Training, 1993. National Report on Australia's Higher Education Sector. Australian Government Publishing Service, Canberra.

Department of Education, Training and Youth Affairs, 2002. Students 2001: Selected Higher Education Statistics. DETYA, Canberra.

Department of Education, Science and Training. 2002. Universities online: a survey of online education and services in Australia, Canberra, March 2002,
www.dest.gov.au/highered/occpaper/02a/ default.htm

Marginson, S, and M. Considine, 2000. The Enterprise University: Power, Governance and Reinvention in Australia, Cambridge University Press, Cambridge.

Masie, E, 2001. Learning Perspectives. TechLearn TRENDS number 202, 14 May. **www.masie.com**

McInnes, C et al, 2000. Trends in the first year experience in Australian universities. Evaluations and Investigations Program 2000/6, Department of Education, Training and Youth Affairs.
www.detya.gov.au/archive/highered/ eippubs/eip00_6/execsum.htm

Oliver, R and Towers, S, 2000. Uptime: students, learning and computers. ICT access and ICT literacy of tertiary students in Australia. Department of Education, Training and Youth Affairs, Canberra.

Red Sheriff, 2001. Australian Internet market is broadening to new audiences. 4 May.
www.redsheriff.com.au/cgi/news.cgi/ Show?_id=6889&sort=TIME&search=

Ryan, Y, 2001. Online education – are universities prepared? Online learning in a borderless market: an exploration of the strategic and policy issues surrounding the growth of e-learning. Evaluations and Investigations Programme, Department of Education, Training and Youth Affairs. February. Forthcoming.

Taylor, JC, 2001. Fifth Generation Distance Education. Keynote address to the 20th World Conference on Open and Distance Education, International Council for Open and Distance Education, Dusseldorf, Germany, 1-5 April 2001

Whyte, A, 2001. Positioning Australian Universities for the 21st Century. Open Learning, Vol.16(1), pp 27-33.

1. University of Technology Sydney

Wiebe Nijlunsing and Jill Armstrong

Context

Three campuses providing locations on both sides of Sydney Harbour comprise the University of Technology Sydney (UTS), the fifth largest university in New South Wales. It grew from a number of smaller teacher education and technical colleges and puts the development of 'professional practice' at the heart of its programmes. 'Almost all undergraduate students are required to have some industrial experience prior to graduation.' Some facts:

- UTS offers around 100 undergraduate degrees and 200 postgraduate courses to more than 27,500 students, including more than 8500 at graduate level. The total number of staff (measured in Full Time Equivalents, FTEs) at UTS in 2001 was 2,183.

- Over a third of UTS students come from a non-English speaking background, up 3% in the last three years. International students represented 19% of commencements and 13% of total enrolments in 2001.

- Over 10,000 students study part-time, nearly 3,000 of those in the Business Faculty.

- As is common in Australian Higher Education a large proportion of students at UTS are studying in their home city. Through a variety of attendance patterns, full-time, part-time and 'sandwich ', UTS offers professionals in the workforce the opportunity to enhance their formal qualifications.

- UTS is the second largest provider of part-time education in Australia. It began to develop distance education in 1996. Its teaching and research programmes are undertaken through the Institute for International Studies and nine Faculties: Business; Design, Architecture and Building; Education; Engineering; Humanities and Social Sciences; Law; Information Technology; Nursing, Midwifery & Health; and Science.

e-Learning and mission

The University of Technology, Sydney is an Australian university with an international focus. It provides higher education to enhance professional practice, to serve the community at large and to enable students to reach their full personal and career potential. The current Strategic Plan at UTS claims a distinctiveness through being 'a pioneer in a new model of education. UTS will be recognised, both nationally and internationally, for its imaginative and dynamic model of practice-based higher education'. In 1996 the opportunity to offer distance-learning courses was enabled through a change in national policy. The same year the Vice-Chancellor announced the 'flexible learning' strategic initiative for the University. 'Our flexible learning environment and effective use of technology in teaching and learning will underpin the university's reputation for excellence in the facilitation of learning and the provision of stimulating and imaginative learning resources'. UTS has put into place reward and recognition policies that reflect the priority given to this aspect of academic work.

Support for teaching and learning

In August 2000, the Institute for Interactive Multimedia (IIM) and the Centre for Learning and Teaching (CLT) formed one unit - the Institute for Interactive Media and Learning (IML). This brought together the staff development for learning and teaching functions with the development of media resources, managing initiatives for online learning and developing courses in interactive multi-media. The IML now sees its role as improving the quality of teaching and learning, with and without the use of technology, developing the UTS website, running post-graduate courses in interactive multimedia and promoting UTS as a centre of excellence in ICT. The IML has a Director, five other academics, three administrative staff and about fourteen web development staff. The Institute will vary in size with various projects etc. that it manages for UTS. Faculties have their own approaches to, and purposes for, the implementation of 'flexible learning'. In support of the flexible learning initiative, top down funds were made available in 1997 to set up six Flexible Action Learning Groups (FLAG). Of the six only the 'Internet Use' FLAG was still functioning in 2002. FLAG bridges the gap between IML and faculties and therefore plays a very important role in dissemination of the outcomes of IML projects and the exchange of good practice of different faculties.

Professor Shirley Alexander who is the Director of the IML, has been involved in supporting the developments in online learning at UTS over many years. She ran the FLAG on Internet Use and led the review and implementation of Computer Mediated Communication (CMC) software which led initially to the use of TopClass. Technical, scaling and software difficulties with TopClass led to a further evaluation and review and the introduction of

Blackboard in 2000. The uptake of CMC and VLE software has travelled in conjunction with the development of online courses at UTS. There seem to be mainly asynchronous Blackboard based online study tools with yet limited content. Reusable courseware, educational simulations, streaming video or synchronous media like video-conferencing, Net-meeting etc. were not mentioned.

Implementation strategy/structure

The short history of distance education at UTS means much online teaching and learning supports campus-based activities. By 2001, 500 courses (modules) involved some online learning. Online courses and support have been growing steadily but are predominantly in a few subject areas. The development of BELL and STAR, two online student support systems, is on going. This is part of the larger UTS Online development. Whilst the IML centrally supports these developments, implementation remains in the hands of faculties and reflects their commitments and needs for 'flexible learning'. UTS is committed to the development of an institutional e-learning strategy. The Quality unit, under Geoff Scott, has done wide-ranging evaluation work on the student experience of e-learning, and have developed a quality framework for its use.

e-Change in the Faculty of Education

The Faculty of Education set up an e-change project in 1999 with the full commitment of the Dean of Education. Whilst initially seeing the project as a cost effectiveness strategy, he discovered that the use of ICT does not make education cheaper but continues to back the project as a means of effectively supporting distance students with opportunities created for opening new distance markets. The project aims to bring the faculty into the UTS online programme, which now uses Blackboard. E-change agents are identified within the faculty and work with other academics on how they wish to develop their own professional practice. The starting point is with the pedagogy and how technology might be used to help support and enhance 'authentic learning'. In 2001 the faculty had 500 students doing some element of their course online. Part of the faculty's work within a national project used a mentoring network for new teachers, using experienced teachers as mentors. This was run from UTS Online and was very successful for those new teachers who were able to get online. This can still be a problem for students, with many not having easy access to computers away from campus and there has not been a particular trend for students to buy their own equipment or get online at home.

Teaching and learning approaches

With its mission directed at 'enhancing professional practice and serving the community at large', much of the learning and teaching focus at UTS is variously described by individuals there as 'work based', 'practice-based' or 'service learning', 'authentic learning' and 'professional practice'. UTS has consistently achieved one of the highest ratings in the level of employability of its graduates. The strategic plan claims, 'the key to our success will be recognition of the legitimacy and value of knowledge creation in professional practice and work settings'. UTS are seeking to create and become renowned for having a 'vibrant learning community' and their plan says:

"Our educational model will focus on the development of autonomous learners, producing graduates who are reflective and creative

practitioners. UTS will be a leader in integrating professional education with workplace and interdisciplinary team experience".

"Our flexible learning environment and effective use of technology in teaching and learning will underpin the University's reputation for excellence in the facilitation of learning and the provision of stimulating and imaginative learning resources".

'Flexible learning' was variously understood within the University as opportunity to study at different times of the day and week facilitated by the use of ICT, through to a view of flexible learning as a new approach to teaching and learning which may include ICT. An example of the latter was provided by Bill Childs, who developed the use of a group space and the file exchange system on Blackboard for small groups of students involved in problem-based learning (joint) assignments. For many across the University however, the journey is still being made towards their own 'versions' of flexible learning and the integration and use of ICT into their courses.

The focus is on 'practice-based' education around which courses are created with students supported online in a variety of ways. Different faculties adapt their own ways of managing their teaching and students learning within the framework of top down support and centralised services. TopClass was used for a range of communication purpose; conferences, online debates, formative assessment, and role-play and simulations. A simulation held across countries and discipline areas has won international recognition for innovation in teaching and learning. Those taking up Blackboard as 'early adopters' of the technology are exploring the potential for new ways of working in teams, group assessment and problem solving.

UTS has undertaken a number of evaluation projects with students to look at how they respond to working online. There is a belief that UTS students' online experiences are very different. In 2001 Shirley Alexander ran a student evaluation across UTS with the intention of developing a set of standards. The Strategic Plan has a target for the same period to work in conjunction with faculties to develop a 'comprehensive e-learning strategy and determine resource and external partnering requirements'.

Staff development

The institutional vision for 'flexible learning' was initiated from top down and was initially financially supported with small grants for development work. A number of Flexible Learning Action Groups were established to look at the range of institutional changes that would facilitate the changes required to implement 'flexible learning'. There was no systematic approach to the development of staff in 'flexible learning' however, but a teaching course for lecturers has been developed, and is available to all staff.

Library

The main task of UTS library is to make resources available to staff and students. The library is not obviously otherwise involved in the education process 'beyond the natural efforts towards illiteracy' and help to use the library functions. The library provides access to almost all resources online, using a management system based on user name/password checked against the university records database.

The library has the controlling authority within the institution for copyright. A recent Digital Copyrights Act has imposed rather limiting restrictions on the multiple use of texts. Only 10% of a book (or other published medium) may be used by the institution just once. (So if teacher A uses chapter one, teacher B cannot use the same chapter and will have to use another source.) Library sorts out if copyright exists for any material a lecturer may want to use and also to seek copyright clearance if it is needed.

Library systems development:

- Direct email contact with a library person/specialist operates on a next-day service. Launching a 24/7 'ask a question live' in conjunction with a Scottish University works on a reciprocal agreement. Response to requests for what resources are held by the library around a particular research issue/question. A discussion is under way to extend this service to IT questions.

- The library and IT services are different units only collaborating at a higher level on a negotiated basis. For any difficulty emerging through firewalls (such as students working in companies might face) other methods are developed.

- Libraries of different universities do not collaborate. Their relationship would be better described as 'co-operation'. Library practice has only just started to reflect on institution policy.

Emerging themes

As in many institutions, there are pockets of innovative practice and excellence with other parts of the institution slower to take on new methods. The prizes won for e-learning evidence this at UTS, and there was clearly a group of early adopters of e-learning practices. Change is a slow cultural process and the top down drive to implement both an e-learning and 'flexible learning' strategy could be seen to have support in a number of areas. As in most places, e-learning opportunities had been developed with greater or lesser success and a maturing process was beginning as a search for quality standards in e-learning. The UTS have taken systematic approaches to reviewing their e-learning developments (UTS Online etc) and technologies and these are slowly making an impact. The UTS focus on 'practice-based learning' and 'authentic learning' is also a theme that resonates with their e-learning developments.

Recommended web-links

UTS has nine faculties, six schools and seven departments, divided over three campuses. See **www.uts.edu.au/about/faculties.html**.

The Institute for Interactive Media and Learning **www.IML.uts.edu.aui**

There is a Blackboard based intranet for the student, called UTS online: **http://online.uts.edu.au/bin/entry_ rightpanel.pl** and for academic staff to get acquainted with Blackboard and to request courses etc: **www.itd.uts.edu.au/flt/admin/** Student administration, module subscription, rostering and study progress monitoring were not explored.

2. University of Wollongong: Flexibility and Creativity

Martin Jenkins and Jan van der Veen

Context

Established in 1951, the University of Wollongong currently offers over 75 undergraduate degrees specialisations and more than 120 postgraduate degrees specialisations to over 13,000 students (of whom more than 2,000 are international students) across nine faculties. Whilst Wollongong does have distance learning courses on campus students are the main focus for the institution.

The University of Wollongong has twice in recent times been awarded Australia's University of the Year; for outstanding research and development partnerships in 1999-2000 and in 2000-2001 for 'Preparing Graduates for the E-World'.

e-Learning and the mission of the university

At Wollongong there is a strong emphasis within university documentation on flexibility in learning and teaching. This emphasis builds from a government contract to deliver distance courses to the south coast area of New South Wales (see South Coast Project mini case study) and from delivery of courses overseas. This work has encouraged flexible development; the emphasis on flexibility is not specifically on the use of technology. The take-up of e-learning has though been rapid, fed by student expectations and by showcasing of other lecturers' work.

The first distance learning developments started with the PAGE project. This was an early 'experiment' with distance learning started at a time when it was recognised that the university was faced with a changing student population. Flexibility in learning and teaching was not articulated until three years ago (1999). PAGE was a post-graduate education project which received AU$3m funding to help set up structures to support distance learning.

e-Learning in the institution is supported through the Academic Services Division which has the following units:

- Centre for Educational Development and Interactive Resources (CEDIR)
- Library
- Learning Development
- Aboriginal Education Centre
- Dean of Students

The responsibility of the Pro Vice-Chancellor Academic (PVC(A)) includes CEDIR, educational policy and off campus learning. At Wollongong off campus activities have proven to be a spur for on campus activity. The PVC(A) role is focused on educational policy, this can be broken down into quality (25%), educational policy (25%) off campus activities (25%) and the rest dealing with issues raised by the university.

Quality audits are being seen as an important driver for change. PVC(A) recognises the value of using these impending visits as important to encourage reflection on teaching practices in preparation for the visits.

Great emphasis is placed on developing graduate attributes and tertiary literacies within students. The focus on graduate attributes and tertiary literacies has a longer history within the institution than its focus on flexibility. There is an information literacy component that is compulsory for all students. They are not specifically linked to the development of flexibility but the importance of the relationship was recognised when developing the policy on flexibility.

Tertiary literacies are mapped to courses, a proforma is used in subject proposals to achieve this mapping.

Implementation strategy & teaching and learning support

The Centre for Educational Development and Interactive Resources (CEDIR) is identified as having an implementation and support role in educational developments and was originally set up to support distance learning. This experience is seen as valuable in underpinning current practice. From these origins CEDIR now has a focus on all academic staff development.

When originally set up CEDIR was self-funding, faculties were charged for the services provided depending on the use made. This was seen as an impediment. CEDIR is now centrally-funded, this release from individual charging is considered a contributory factor to the rapid increase in demand for CEDIR services. Priorities are identified through Faculty Service Agreements (FSA), introduced in 1999, agreed with each faculty. Originally all requests went via the PVC (A) office but this was seen to be political so was changed to bring in the FSA. Any service can be covered by the FSA (requests can be for multimedia, video etc), educational developers discuss with Deans their focus on subjects and the Dean signs off that list. Applying for time through the FSA is also applied internally to ASC.

In its earlier days CEDIR worked with individual academics, it has now moved to working at Faculty level, focusing on subjects. The University of Wollongong has Faculty Education Committees; it was one of the first universities to do this. They report to the University Education Committee. Having the Faculty Education Committees has helped the process of CEDIR consultation. Working at course level was not considered to be effective as it was difficult to maintain one responsible course leader due to staff turnover. The practice is now to deal with subject co-ordinators. Problems with changing roles and staff turnover can also result in subject co-ordinators changing but the emphasis on the subject does result in a clear message that the subject is owned by the University and not by the individual; this is seen as important. Once a subject area has been identified through the discussions with the faculty then CEDIR staff will discuss with individual staff the work involved.

The advantages of this approach from CEDIR have been that it is the lecturer who decides on the priorities and that allows better planning and allocation of resources. This does though demand clear project management to ensure that all the necessary information is at hand and control is maintained over the developments. To ensure this, they have developed their own database, which produces reports on projects. This also acts as a form of publicity, promoting within the university what is going on in other faculties, which helps stimulate interest.

A recent approach taken with academics is to focus on 'learning objects' as opposed to whole courses; this could include individual lectures or modules. This smaller scale approach is seen as being successful. The hope also is that these 'objects' can then be shared. They are investigating how these 'objects' can be tagged so that they can be identified and reused elsewhere.

The unit have a pragmatic approach to developments, recognising the need for revision and evaluation. They expect to have a three-year life cycle for projects. Originally 140 hours were offered for development, with production starting six months before delivery. Starting this far in advance was a big change for many academics who were more used to just-in-time preparation. Given the three-stage cycle, 140 hours were offered in the first year; 70 hours in the second;

and ten hours in the third year. It has been found though that 140 hours was too much and this is no longer offered. Focus of developments is now on developing smaller units.

A more recent mechanism for CEDIR to become engaged in discussions with staff is through the Initial Tertiary Teaching programme on which all new academic staff are enrolled. Whilst all new staff have to enroll on the programme they do not have to complete. The issue of compulsion, making staff complete this programme is an 'issue' within the university at the present. The ITT programme is seen as an important development as it integrates online teaching into staff development as a whole.

SOS is an online survey tool that CEDIR have developed. It is an e-mail driven system and all responses are anonymous. The system contains a number of databases containing different questions which the lecturer can then select from, or if they want create their own. The system provides a quick way for lecturers to get feedback and experience shows that online surveys have a lower return but the data is much richer.

Teaching and learning approaches

The range of use of e-learning within the University includes supplementary, complementary and online approaches. Delivery to campus-based students being more supplementary or complementary. It is Wollongong's intention to audit how e-learning is used within the institution; it is recognised that much is still text based information delivery with not much multimedia or collaborative learning developments. Distance learning courses can be online or with examples from the courses delivered overseas by the Faculty of Education include a hybrid approach making use of both CD-ROM and Internet. The examples below illustrate specific examples within the university:

> **South Coast Arts Project Case Study**
> The South Coast Arts project is government funded. It provided an opportunity for the development of provision to education outreach centres. Flexibility is provided through the choice of number of modules taken each year. Once started on a module the students work through as a cohort, there is not flexibility in terms of pace of learning.
>
> The project has identified differences in perception of experience between on campus and off campus students. Each group perceives that the other group has some advantage; for example off campus students perceive on campus students have better library provision compared to their local centres. On campus students perceive that off campus students have better IT access.
>
> Library provision at the centres on the south coast is small and very focused. The emphasis has been on e-provision, the set-up for library provision was AU$0.5m. These developments have though benefited on campus students as well. The experiences that are coming out of this project will feed into provision for on campus students. The perspective taken was to set up an infrastructure that could support many.
>
> Outcomes to date from the project show from a learning development perspective the important issues are not content related but skills related; evaluation, group work, discussion etc. In terms of the academic staff the biggest conceptual leap has been moving staff from content to process focus. The project has also highlighted the importance of collaboration between different units; CEDIR, library, subject co-ordinators.

Active Health site - Web site has been set up with a view to whether such a site can contribute to the development of a community of professional association. The site is aimed at physical educators.
(www.activehealth.uow.edu.au)

The main body of the site consists of resources for physical educators i.e. teaching supports, lesson ideas, online learning activities, literature reviews. The resources are suggested by participants/students - suggestions are reviewed before being added to the site. The next stage is to try and develop the community.

Maths project – 123 count with me. Internal project for use in Wollongong, used with remote teachers to provide guidance on setting up a classroom, includes text and multimedia resources based on a 3D world. Also incorporates wizards to help the teacher develop activities for individual children based on student profiles that can be built up through the resource.

Technical support

The Learning Online Team (LOL) within CEDIR supports the creation and development of WebCT units within the University. The Learning Online Team have identified their customers as:

- Subject co-ordinators (primary client), these identified staff have responsibility for WebCT units once set up. Requests for sites are only accepted through subject co-ordinators, these individuals will have had WebCT training. The subject co-ordinators are responsible for copyright, privacy issues, content etc. Student additions are also the responsibility of the subject co-ordinators.

- Faculty staff (support staff)

- On campus students

- Off campus students

- Overseas students, though a small proportion of LOL customers providing support to this group can be very time consuming.

Current levels of WebCT use are 750 sites (approx 375 per semester) with 10k students having access during 2001. It is expected that the number of sites will exceed 800 during 2002. WebCT is also used for training and project support

The resources LOL have developed to help them in their role include a student database, subject database, staff directory and their own LOL database. These databases allow tracking of the sites historically, including information such as who owns intellectual property rights.

The process of WebCT site creation starts with a subject co-ordinator making contact with an educational developer. Requests are submitted to LOL using a web-based site establishment notification
(http://130.130.140.18/WebCT/delivery.html). In the early stages of WebCT developments all courses were automatically set up, now that a critical mass has been achieved some proposals are not developed. LOL do have concerns about how they will manage the dramatic increase in demand for courses. In terms of real changes in teaching and learning they estimate that there will be three cycles before the use of WebCT is fully integrated into the teaching.

The team feel they have an obligation for quality assurance to ensure consistency for students. For example they have developed faculty templates, which are consistent with the second level within WebCT. These templates include generic links and in-built help. Icons are provided on the web in faculty colours that can be downloaded (consistent symbols are used throughout). With the growing demand for WebCT units they recognise that they cannot have control of all courses set up. Longer term they see peer review and outside quality audits as the main drivers for maintaining quality.

Once the site establishment notification comes through a new site is created or a copy made of one used previously. The primary designer is then notified and a dummy user created. The LOL team also pick up the student cohort data and add students. These students are then added to a control group that is updated daily. Students are registered using an automatic e-mail account they are set up with, this does restrict who can be added and can cause some problems with overseas students. LOL manually archive sites and then take them off line when complete.

The LOL support site (see recommended web-links) provides support information for both staff and students. The LOL students' web page allows students to check if they are registered. Student inductions are provided for off campus students but not comprehensively provided for on campus; though this activity is growing. Educational developers will run sessions with lecturers, especially those who lack some confidence in the use of WebCT.

A staff survey of usage will now be done on an annual basis, this will ask what tools are being used and show the level of, and pattern of, use. The survey is showing that WebCT is being used for a wide range and increasing number of functions. Feedback also suggests that it is becoming fundamental to the running of courses.

A recent development is the creation of electronic readings within courses, and print materials that have been scanned. This process is administered through the copyright service in the library. Subject co-ordinators provide a list of citations to the library; the LOL team then takes over the process of getting them into WebCT.

If the articles are available online then the approach taken is to direct the student to the resource rather than provide a direct link to the specific item. A resource database is maintained so they have a record of readings, for sharing, but also this enables the lists to be made available on the web and not just hidden within WebCT courses.

Research and development: Applied research and creative design

In the Faculty of Education research and development with respect to the instrumentation of education takes place. Besides the faculty staff, also staff members of other units (CEDIR, Creative Arts, Informatics,) and students of the Masters program on IT in education are involved in what is called the Research Centre for Interactive Learning Environments (RILE) and the Digital Media Centre (DMC). Both PhD and professional doctorates can be applied for within this context. Besides other topics such as interactive TV and video, research focuses on the improvement of the learning designs for online learning and the development of reusable templates for successful examples (in collaboration with Edith Cowan University). Within this project they found four key principles for quality designs:

- engage learners;

- acknowledge context;

- challenge learners; and

- provide practice.

Research into the development of reusable learning design templates has evaluated over 50 exemplars. From these evaluations four learning design templates have been identified:

- Rule based learning design;
  - The learning design focus is to apply standard procedures and rules in a solution;
- Incident based learning design;
  - The learning design focus is to reflect and make decisions based on actions and events;
- Strategy based learning design;
  - The learning design focus is to develop strategy; tasks require strategic planning;
- Role based learning design;
  - The learning design focus is to understand the issues, processes and interactions of complex, non-predictive situations by participating as a player in a setting which models a real world application.

Developmental work and associated research takes place in the context of what is called the EMLab (Educational Media Lab). EMLab was created in the early 1990s and has been successful in generating income to cover costs of the staff and in gathering awards for the multimedia resources developed on a wide range of topics (interactive Opera House, Olympic games, Maths,). Developments have been predominantly CD-based, but they now moving to online. However a hybrid approach is still common with browser based materials produced on CDs in recognition of access problems. Online access is thus used for mentoring and checking.

Analysis and emerging issues

This section combines a discussion of emerging themes identified and commented upon by the visiting group. The following is, therefore, a combination of information found and opinions of the visitors:

- The University of Wollongong has so far managed to implement a high percentage of its courses in WebCT in a coordinated and supportive way. It will be important to proceed in ways that are sustainable for those who are doing the support, while maintaining a level of flexibility for both students and staff. So far the University of Wollongong has shown that it has the culture and the means to do so. Resources however are stretched with both multimedia production facilities and interactive learning environment support in place.

- Within the R&D context it was clear that researchers in their role as teachers are not likely to comply with constraints that online learning environments impose on teachers. They are always on the move to further improvements and new options. The way ahead appears to be that emphasis should be placed on designing rich learning experiences while offering simple technical solutions to support that. For the University of Wollongong it is a rich environment to have both a support centre (CEDIR) and input from research and development programs in the Faculty of Education of University of Wollongong, both showing great creativity in their approaches and designs.

- Reusability of content is an emerging issue found both within the research and the implementation settings. This issue involves technical solutions such as templates for learning design and repositories for units of learning material. However, human aspects have also to be considered so as to ensure that intended users (teachers) perceive and receive the benefits planned for.

Recommended web-links

University of Wollongong
www.uow.edu.au

CEDIR
http://cedir.uow.edu.au

Learning and Teaching Strategic Plan
**www.uow.edu.au/about/teaching/
LTStrategic_plan.html**

Learning Online Team
www.uow.edu.au/LOL/

Educational Multimedia lab (emlab)
www.emlab.uow.edu.au/

Digital media centre
www.digitalmedia.uow.edu.au/

Research Centre for Interactive Learning
Environments (RILE)
www.uow.edu.au/educ/rdcentres/rile/

3. Charles Sturt University: Everything depends on whether it will scale

Robert Harding and Helen McEvoy

Context

Charles Sturt University (CSU) was formed in 1989 from the amalgamation of the Riverina Murray Institute of Higher Education and the Mitchell College of Advanced Education at Bathurst. The University has a number of campuses in New South Wales; in size order – Wagga Wagga (half way between Sydney and Melbourne), Bathurst (200km west of Sydney), Albury (300km north of Melbourne) and lesser ones at Dubbo and Goulburn. Covering a vast geographical area, CSU has had to develop effective mechanisms to cope with such a distributed campus – it is 500 km from Bathurst to Albury and CSU has its own microwave links.

Partly driven by geographical imperatives, CSU's mission has historically involved the delivery of higher education through distance education both nationally and internationally. This has led to an early commitment to the use of ICT in programme delivery and their claim to providing the most extensive online support in Australia of distance education courses. Delivery methods can therefore be said to be dual mode with high commitment to ongoing paper delivery.

CSU's policies also need to be seen in the context of its founding partners' missions to serve the economically-oriented educational needs of its regions. Partnerships are important, and they result in up to 50% funding of some courses (Police Academy, Ministry of Agriculture, Australian wine industry). Few partnerships have been formed directly with industry: most are with non-profit organisations and the public sector. The courses run by CSU tend to reflect regional interests, partnership arrangements, and vocational courses. CSU has no law, medicine or engineering, but has a centre of excellence in viticulture, an equine centre, and has courses in nursing, paramedic studies, and irrigation (half a chair in Irrigation is paid for by the New South Wales Dept of Water).

CSU currently has 30,000 students enrolled across campuses (14,000 full-time equivalents). Of these, some 22,000 are registered as distance education students of which: 12,000 are from Sydney, Wollongong and Newcastle, 5,000 are from the rest of mainland Australia and 5,000 are offshore students. By 2003, to enroll, students will be required to have the use of a PC. A recent survey showed that 90% of current students have ready access to a computer and 70% have Internet access.

e-Learning and the mission of the university

CSU made the decision to 'go electronic' because the technology offers the prospect of improved levels of service to its widespread student body. Its regulations, however, stipulate that printing costs shall not be passed on to students, which means that students expect printed materials to be included in their course fees and so CSU cannot just stop providing printed materials without cutting its fees. It is thus denied one of the obvious cost benefits of going electronic and must look to other factors for the business case for electronic learning.

The process began about five years ago. There are approximately 2500 courses (subjects as CSU calls them) and it was not feasible to rewrite them all for electronic delivery. CSU began by simply scanning in the pre-existing paper-based materials and making these available electronically alongside the printed materials. Newer courses are being developed in the electronic format, the print version being produced from that.

33

Centre for Enhancing and Learning Teaching (CELT)

Petrina Quinn, Director of CELT, presented the work of her Unit. CELT was set up to play a leading role in the development of learning and teaching within the University by:

- developing learning resources for on campus and distributed education teaching using a variety of media;

- providing a range of academic staff development activities and an Evaluation Unit.

The Centre itself is made up of two directorial staff, a two-person evaluation unit, and a team of twenty educational designers with dedicated 'school' responsibilities. This large team 'is committed to the development of quality learning resources using all appropriate media, supported by relevant communications technology.' (www.csu.edu.au/division/celt/html/ services.html)

CELT has built a very large and highly scalable online environment, initially based on existing resources and featuring a highly integrated course administration structure. This they have designed and produced themselves; they do not at present use a proprietary e-Learning platform (though Blackboard is under consideration). Every student has access to this environment, described by Petrina as an 'Enterprise solution', through a portal called 'myCSU'. It provides access to:

- eBox – for administrative transactions

- course materials;

- forums;

- on-Line chat facilities;

- links;

- EASTS – CSU's electronic evaluation tracking system.

The lessons learned from their experience are summed up by Petrina Quinn:

- Content is good but communication is everything;

- Scalability is everything;

- Nothing scales like automation.

This reflects CSU's shift from teaching to learning and a move from dual-mode to multi-mode learning (on campus, partnerships, workplace-based learning, distributed education, and access centres).

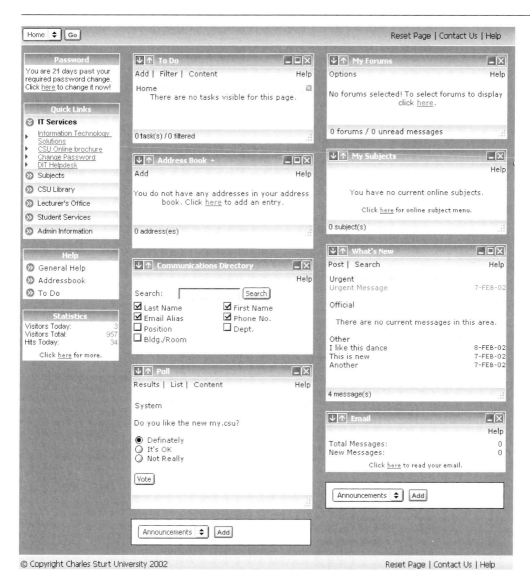

Figure 1: Screen shot of MyCSU

Implementation strategy

The main issues apart from sheer quantity of content, are staff development and the need to identify appropriate pedagogic strategies. There is a staff development programme that includes a full semester's training for new academic staff into teaching and learning in the e-learning environment, but we were not able to judge how CSU is approaching the question of pedagogic strategies.

An educational designer is assigned to each Faculty at the rate of about 1 per 20 academic staff. They are the key to providing a 'delivery solution' for a course, liaising with academics to define course content and then taking responsibility for managing the production of course materials such as print, video and audio materials.

Student admissions and automated administrative processes

Ian McDermott outlined CSU's development and implementation of online administrative processes - admissions, timetabling, examination administration and finance (student records are not available online). For students and staff, McDermott believes online administration processes will give the user control over their teaching and learning experience. So committed is CSU to online administration that it is anticipated, by 2003, enrolment criteria will include having access to a computer and the Internet.

Teaching and learning approaches

With the introduction of electronic delivery CSU's Vice-Chancellor required an electronic forum to be set up for all subjects. In principle, this provides a means of interaction between all students on a given course and their lecturers.

We learned, however, that a study approximately three years after implementation showed that less than 10% of these forums were being used for 'good' educational purposes and 70% were not being used at all. CSU, we were told is "struggling to find pedagogic models that fit with forums". Thus we are led to observe that apart from putting resources on the web and using the web for administration and course production, CSU's approach to teaching and learning is mostly traditional.

Library

Library services and collections are provided at Wagga Wagga, Bathurst, and Albury Wodonga. At the newest site, Dubbo, library facilities and resources are accessible via online facilitated access.

The library aims to provide equity of access to services and resources through a combination of physical and electronic services to duplicate the on campus experience for off campus users.

Remote access is via:

- a free call number;
- post;
- email or fax;
- an electronic link to library services provided on MyCSU.

Services and resources include:

- posting of monographs and videos within mainland Australia (student pays return postage);
- printed and electronic document delivery – there are issues around electronic document delivery – the student would be liable for printing costs;

- online databases and e-journals;
- Ask a Librarian reference enquiry service;
- Web-ezy – a self-paced interactive tutorial for the development of library and information skills.

CSU is undergoing a review of the executive structure of the university. Currently, Library Services is under the Pro Vice-Chancellor (Public Affairs), but will soon be answerable to the Deputy Vice-Chancellor (Administration). This new structure will bring Library Services into the same division as such diverse departments as Legal Services, Information Technology and University Properties.

Historically, the library is part of a group called the Integrated Learning Systems Group (ILSG) which is answerable to the Pro Vice-Chancellor (Planning and Development). This group has been very influential in forming the direction of future ICT developments within the university, whether administrative or more directly relating to teaching and learning. This group comprises the DIT, CELT and the library – there is no direct academic involvement.

Relationships and partnerships

Course partnerships

CSU engages extensively in 'third-party franchises' between itself and other educational institutions. There are two models of international partnerships with regard to their courses. The first is the 'affiliated college model', the second the 'one-to-one model'. For the first, CSU works with an overseas institution that wants to offer some of their courses or programmes to its own students. The model involves CSU providing the learning materials (print and online), the teaching expertise, and standardised assessment and leads

to a CSU degree being awarded. The second model is the 'one-to-one model', in which CSU supplies everything, and the off-shore group is treated as distributed education students. There is a major partnership with the School of Professional and Continuing Education in Hong Kong of this nature, for both IT programmes and library science.

Research partnerships

Research and development relationships with external funding involve the university as a partner contributing 'in kind'. One example involves the Farrier Centre (http://farrier.csu.edu.au/), a research centre for agriculture. The Centre itself is funded by the university, but serves as a unit to bring in projects and funding from industry and government partners. Faculty members can 'claim' funding support from the Centre for research based on their input, such as the number of 'points' earned for publishing articles in scientific journals. The funding support is mainly to fund Masters and PhD students.

Another example is the 'Rice' Project, in which the partners include the 'Rice-Growers Co-operative'. There are one or two other universities involved and also various government units (see www.ricecrc.org/). This seven-year project provides enough money to support 15 Masters students and 15 PhD students, (supporting a PhD student means paying the tuition, fees and giving the student $AU 20,000 per year stipend). The graduate students present their work each year to a colloquium, where they are questioned extensively by rice farmers themselves, as to the applicability of their research. If a consortium wants to re-apply after seven years, they must select a new set of issues.

The HSC Online Project

Lyn Gorman, Head of School, School of Humanities and Social Sciences, is Director of the 'NSW HSC online project'. 'HSC' is the Higher Schools Certificate for which secondary school pupils in NSW prepare. Lyn developed some materials for the original site (there is now a second generation).

The HSC Project is the brainchild of a CSU Pro Vice-Chancellor: he was helping his daughter to locate educational resources over the web and realised that CSU had a role to play in secondary education. This is an example of the context of its founding partners' missions (to serve the economically-oriented educational needs of its regions) already noted. The project is a joint institutional project run mainly by DET (The State of NSW's Dept of Education and Training).

The HSC site provides resources for Rural & Regional communities. The state Board of Studies is responsible for examination setting, and supports this project. HSC site content has links back to syllabuses and past papers on the Board's site. All content is directly relevant to syllabus for year 11 and 12 students (i.e. 16, 17 year olds). CSU provides technological support, and in the first phase members of the University contributed to the content development. In the second generation there's a clearer split of work: content is written by teachers on day release funded by DET.

There is some crossover with CSU's main programme. The Bachelor of Media Communications programme is using the web technology and the within-institution relationships evolved under the HSC Project to put in place the structure for delivering the course online.

Analysis and emerging issues

- Decisions made with regard to the implementation of e-learning strategies primarily appear to be made with regard to cost and efficiency savings rather than to any commitment to improve teaching and learning from a pedagogical basis.

- There is evidence here for the way that Universities may react to new circumstances: e.g. to the increasing commercialisation/ commoditisation of education. There is a threat to institutions like CSU from 'tiering', e.g. Private Universities, perhaps in alliance with major commercial partners, may cream off some traditional 'constituents'. There is also evidence that commercialisation leads to the downplay of the academics' contribution.

- Emphasis appears to be on the introduction of a electronic learning environment to provide efficiencies and to improve student access and communication. Again, the advantages from a teaching and learning perspective remain unclear.

- 'Universities will be differentiated not by the content they deliver but by the service they deliver' – Leslie Burr (Manager CSU Online)

- Confusion as to the role of academic teaching staff. Academic staff consider themselves to have been marginalised, particularly in terms of consultation and decision making. Additionally, there is some feeling that the university centres on administrative processes, and those that provide these services over the core teaching and learning services, and those that provide the latter.

- Resolving the 'everything must be in print format as well as online' issue.

- The main driver for CSU seems to be the need to achieve efficiency through economies of scale, fuelled by a drive to reduce fees and increase service.

Recommended web-links

Charles Sturt University homepage
www.csu.edu.au/

MyCSU web page
www.csu.edu.au/division/studserv/ online/mycsu.htm

CELT web page
www.csu.edu.au/division/celt/

Home page for HSC Online
http://hsc.csu.edu.au/study/

The distance education service at CSU's home page
www.csu.edu.au/study/de.html

CSU handbook for current and previous years
www.csu.edu.au/handbook/

The Learning Materials web page
www.csu.edu.au/division/lmc/?cssc.htm

CSU assessment draft policy
www.csu.edu.au/acadman/assessment-draft2.htm

Inaugural CELT Learning and Teaching forum Re-examining Learning and Teaching at CSU.

This paper results from the inaugural CELT Learning and Teaching forum and identifies issues, makes recommendations and evaluates the forum
www.csu.edu.au/division/OLI/pubs/occpap/ no21/celt/

Leslie Burr, Manager CSU Online, presentation discussing a university wide systematic approach to web publishing.
www.gu.edu.au/conference/educause2001/ content2a.html

Inventing a Better Mouth Trap: The Development and Implementation of Forum Software at Charles Sturt University. Article by Leslie Burr, Manager CSU Online discussing large-scale solutions for the development and implementation of online forums.
http://ausweb.scu.edu.au/aw01/papers/ refereed/burr/paper.html

Measuring Students' Use of Electronic Books. By Dr John Messing, School of Information Studies, CSU. An older paper (1995) examining methods to enable measuring use of electronic books.
www.ascilite.org.au/conferences/melbourne 95/smtu/papers/messing.pdf

Learning to Learn Online. Paper presented by E. Smith at the Ascilite conference, Brisbane 1999, on the results of a piloted supplementary subject run in 1999, called, Skills for Learning Online.
www.ascilite.org.au/conferences/brisbane 99/papers/smith.pdf

Enhancing Student Learning Through Online Support. Paper presented by Gary Williams, Bill Lord, and Mark McFadden, CELT, Open Learning Institute, CSU. The paper relates to trialing the delivery of online supported subjects in 1997 and describes: design and development aspects, support mechanisms, evaluation and outcomes.
www.ascilite.org.au/conferences/perth97/ papers/Williams/Williams.html

Tools for authoring Constructivist Computer Assisted Learning Resources: A review. Paper presented by Barney Dalgarno, School of Information Studies, CSU. This Ascilite Conference paper reviews possible tools for authoring constructivist computer assisted resources.
www.ascilite.org.au/conferences/ wollongong98/asc98-pdf/dalgarno0153.pdf

'An evaluation of an alternative delivery system in the school of education at Charles Sturt University.' David H McKinnon, Dieter Opfer, Mark McFadden
www.ascilite.org.au/conferences/ wollongong98/asc98-pdf/mckinnon.pdf

The office of the Vice-Chancellor. Unfortunately, not all the site has enabled access, but it is useful in that it shows strategic plans for different divisions.
http://louisewww.mit.csu.edu.au/division/vc office/strategic.html

'A decision making simulation using computer mediated communication'. Article by Robert McLaughlan, University of Technology, Sydney and Denise Kirkpatrick, CELT, CSU.
http://cleo.murdoch.edu.au/ajet/ajet15/ mclaughlan.html

4. Southern Cross University: Flexibility and Quality

Martin Valcke and Jan van der Veen

Context

Originally founded as a college of advanced education (CAE), and later integrated into the University of New England, the institute is now an independent regional university since 1994 and operates in one main and three smaller campuses. Recent growth in student numbers was generated in the region. Now, about 10,000 students are enrolled in a wide variety of programmes. This number of students represents about 5000 full-time student equivalents. About 54% of the students are external and take courses in a variety of distance education modes, which includes services at the smaller campuses. Distance education students tend to be in the main female, 35+ and responsible for their families. A national quality review of higher education institutes in Australia revealed that Southern Cross University scored very high on 'student satisfaction', reflecting the high degree of teacher-student interaction, student support and the quality of the teaching. This survey also included the opinions of the large group of distance education students.

The mission of SCU is grounded in delivering education for the region. Next to this, the university has a high profile in setting up very innovative programmes that are closely linked to economical/societal needs of the region; such as Natural resources, Forestry, Tourism and Agribusiness. Other approaches build on developing niche market courses/programmes such as Naturopathy, Contemporary Music and Indigenous Studies. The staff reflects a young profile, which helps to adopt innovative ideas. Now, the student population is not expected to grow, considering students are funded with public money. Student growth is expected in external students (e.g., Singapore and Sweden).

The business model for the latter is based on overseas partnerships. Education is delivered to overseas students through partner institutions that provide local tutors, there is an e-mail relationship and an Australian lecturer/tutor/unit assessor would visit the site and teach a full day, then the local institute takes over. To guarantee quality, 20 to100% of the assessment is controlled by SCU. Overseas students receive SCU-certificates.

e-Learning and the mission of the university

The university mission stresses 'flexible learning'. This central concept is the central argument to choose for e-learning, online solutions and affects nearly all other strategic and educational decisions. The prime focus of setting up flexible learning is to attain quality, not the enrolment of large numbers of new students although SCU staff become able to do so.

From 1996 on, top management of the university have stressed and pushed the use of online provisions in the educational design of all the courses as a particular interpretation of the concept of flexible learning. This central directive was, to a certain extent, in conflict with very different interpretations of the concept in educational designers and academic staff.

After 4 years of implementating online provisions, the following picture can be drawn. About 340 units of 700 units of study have a clear ICT link.

- 54% of the courses are only reflected at a basic level in the portal environment;
- 7% of the courses are fully online;
- 11% of the courses are web-dependent; and
- 29% is web-supplemented.

Choice for students is important (print, e-mail, online,). They can decide to take a course along a certain mode. The restricted bandwith of the university and the private telephone lines cause difficulties to implement very advanced online provisions. As to the learning materials; a majority of the learning materials is print based. Overseas student receive less support. Recent restructuring tries to solve resource issues to meet the specific demands of distance education students.

Teaching and Learning Centre

A key player in the University is the Teaching and Learning Centre (TLC). This support group is active in supporting every school of the university and responsible for the educational design of the courses. Next to support services, they set up their own research programme. The centre plays a role in the development of policies of the university. The recent Quality audits of the university help to develop new policies to answer new needs. TLC builds its strategy on the strategies of the schools. It urges these schools to develop their own strategy. TLC, for example, does not impose a specific educational model; it especially helps to make explicit the model the individual/school wants to adopt.

TLC now documents and materializes its expertise. A key document is The Flexible Learning Quality Guide (FLQG). For the different sections in this Guide, templates are available.

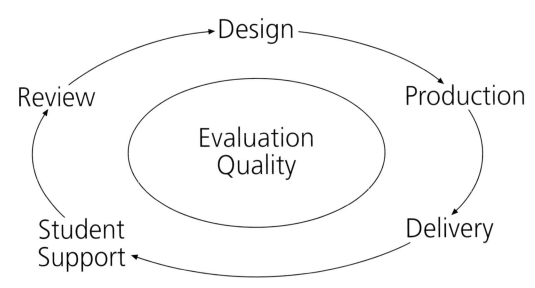

Figure 2

There is no teaching/learning plan at university level. TLC has to operate outside an available framework. Example: the moving away from norm referenced to criterion referenced testing started by TLC and is now official university policy for graduate courses.

TLC also promotes staff development in a variety of fields:

- How to prepare for a quality audit.

- How to use generic forums.

- How to set up external peer review.

- How to become an interactive teacher online.

- Research meetings (topics about T&L).

- Getting people to start research projects about issues in teaching & learning.

In order to enhance staff teaching skills, a 'Graduate certificate in teaching in higher education' is offered, in particular to new staff members.

Implementation strategy

All students have been online since July 2000. But, the current approach builds on a slow start-up phase. Initially, Learning Space was adopted with limited technical support and this was not taken up well. A review of available solutions on the e-learning market focused on finding a transparent system (not a Porsche, not a 4 wheel drive) and Blackboard was adopted. The implementation is mainly supported by the IT section. Stronger ties with TLC are strived for.

Key issues in the implementation strategies:

- Next to the online staff and student portals (MySCU, see Figure 3), the university also completely re-developed its own administrative support system.

- Everyone is online.

- It is an integration of a personalised, single logon portal and Blackboard-tools (forum, agenda,); middleware was developed to connect all services.

- 'Consistency' is pursued from a student/staff point of view.

- Strong link with student administration.

- Injection of hardware provisions on campus.

- Teachers that had dedicated Web-sites in place before Blackboard was adopted, can stick to their solutions, but are asked to integrate this with the portal and use the available tool.

- Two schools received extra money to set up online courses.

- Extra support for teachers: introductory three-hour session, hands-on two hour refresher course, dedicated e-mail link to give support (always someone on duty)/ call centre;

- All menu-options in Blackboard are by default disabled. Based on the course design staff can switch on options.

The university is now in a phase where they have to influence the late- and non-adopters. This remains a difficulty. Another problem is the sustainability of the number of support provisions. A model with a keyperson/super user in each Faculty is being considered.

Because of the limited availability and the high costs of bandwith to the Internet a protocol is in place for both staff and students which combines limitations with respect to session length and the maximum amount of Mb that can be retrieved from the Internet.

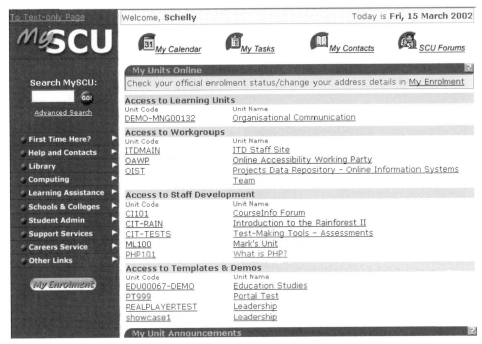

Figure 3: The portal of Southern Cross University: MySCU.

Teaching and learning approaches

A key cornerstone of the teaching and learning approaches is the adoption of Improved Assessment Practices. With a grant from the government, current assessment procedures were reviewed and new approaches were developed in an operational way: self assessment, peer assessment, This is reflected in publications of the centre (e.g., Chris Morgan & Meg O'Reilley, Assessing open and distance learners, London: Kogan Page; and a forthcoming publication The Assessment Handbook). The development and use of a Student Feedback System is in line with this cornerstone. Although not mandatory, about 2/3 of the staff/students use it. With respect to student skills, educational programmes focus on getting employable by learning in authentic settings.

The library

The library is positioned very close to the client (students, academics). The library policy is clearly faculty driven and fits into the educational system in a number of ways:

- Academics determine the acquisition of books and journals.

- There are library representatives on all boards of faculties.

- There are lots of informal meetings.

- Librarians help with getting references into Blackboard(Bb) supported courses.

- Staff are involved in faculty projects to help get resources online.

- 'Online literacy skills': how to use library catalogue, how to access vendors, databases, how to use internet for research, library website.

The library is spread over three campuses and services on and off campus students via one helpdesk which supports IT and Blackboard questions at the same time. It focuses on the acquisition of electronic sources (digital, networkable etc.). There is a web-based Document Supply Service, a 0800 toll free number and a service called 'Ask a librarian online'. The catalogue system, Unilink, is shared with other Australian universities. Additionally the library supplies a copyright advice service and a limited copyright clearance service.

The directions to go for the library are:

- more digital materials and online publishing;
- more computers;
- involvement of staff in teaching;
- involvement in research.

Analysis and emerging issues

The visit to SCU revealed a number of issues. The elaboration builds on the interviews, observations and discussions with SCU-staff, but also includes comments and information brought into this set by the EC visitors:

- SCU was clearly an example of an institute that puts 'teaching and learning' very central in its programme. Although not a formal overall institutional policy to ground this education is available, the elaborated collaboration between central and de-central institutes (schools, colleges) seems to induce medium- and long-term perspectives.

- Interviews with staff members of colleges and schools present a very independent picture of what teaching, learning, ICT, assessment, should look like. But, in general, the 'independent' ideas being presented still seem to reflect basic ideas supported by central policies and the central Teaching and Learning Centre.

- SCU clearly adopts a distinct approach to the concept of distance education when we consider overseas students. To the institute they are distant; but to the students this might not be true. They enroll in local institutions – within the context of a partnership with SCU – and take courses. But in general this might be again in a face-to-face context with local tutors and print-based materials involved. The SCU-perspective is especially reflected in the way the learning materials are being developed: as flexible, re-usable sets of materials by other institutes, partners etc.

- The library supplies SCU with a very intelligently planned, well co-ordinated library and information service, making appropriate use of electronic learning technologies. There seems to be a real attempt to be actively involved in the forward planning of future services through full participation in the online committees (the university's mechanism for planning, implementation and evaluation).

- Forthcoming new priorities, research and connections with the professions, compete with ICT in education as staff workload has its limitations.

5. Queensland University of Technology: The real world meets the virtual world

Rhonda Riachi and Annette Roeters

Context

Queensland University of Technology (QUT) is one of Australia's largest universities, enrolling over 30,000 students in the fast growing city of Brisbane. QUT was established in 1989, formerly an Institute of Technology. At that time research was a distant vision, but they developed this in selective subjects and also built on their strong teaching reputation.

QUT comprises nine faculties across three Brisbane campuses, and offers a broader range of undergraduate degrees than most other universities, with the flexibility to choose a combination of study areas as well as participate in exchange programmes with overseas universities. The Faculties are Built Environment and Engineering, Business, Creative Industries, Education, Health, Humanities and Human Science, Information Technology, Law and Science.

QUT is the largest provider of bachelor degree graduates into full-time employment in Australia each year and its graduate employment rate is well above the national average for Australian universities. Mature students comprise 40% of the intake and overseas students 10%. Less than 50% of the university's funding comes from government, the rest from fee-paying students and about 10% from external sources.

University approach to e-Learning

The senior management view is that the advance of 'borderless education' will make the distinctions between academic education and professional education, between certificate and portfolio, and between campus-based and online learning increasingly meaningless. Students will have a different relationship with the campus, not either one or the other. It is therefore not surprising that proficiency in using ICT for learning is one of the key 'generic capabilities' that QUT aims to develop in all students over their course of study.

However, the university remains a local campus-based university by choice, with only a few strategically chosen initiatives for external provision of courses. They include targeting the IT market in Singapore (the biggest market for online degrees), and nursing and professional development in other Asian countries. Of the 256 degrees on offer, 6 are totally online. There is an Online Teaching (OLT) steering committee with representatives from each faculty, and all efforts in this area are supported by the Teaching and Learning Support Service (TaLSS).

Support for teaching and learning

In 1992 QUT established a Teaching and Learning Committee, chaired by the Deputy Vice-Chancellor with Associate Deans of Teaching comprising the members. It established an internal grants scheme with criteria for bidding. To avoid 'boutique' technical developments (where initiatives fail to join with others or adopt strategic aims) they have moved to a faculty focus for the bids, and do not accept bids from individuals.

The grants are used mostly for time release for academics, and development time for IT or possibly a research assistant, but they are not research grants. Project reports are sent to two members of the T&L committee to review and they report back to the committee on whether the project outcomes have been achieved. Some areas are specified each year for development. These are related to QUT's strategic priorities for teaching and learning:

- Generic graduate capabilities.

- Flexible learning technologies.

- Improving assessment.

- Indigenous perspectives in the curriculum.

- Internationalisation of the curriculum.

The T&L committee oversees the work of TaLSS, the department which brings together a range of academic support services:

- Software and multimedia integrated learning environment (SMILE) – 30 staff led by Halima Goss.

- Open learning – 15 staff working on mainly paper-based materials;

- Educational TV – supporting a public TV station run by students.

- Student support and systems – frontline support for student enquiries, including provision of an ISP for students.

- AV and photography services.

- The Hub – a new initiative incorporating support for teaching evaluation, teaching and learning grants, and a teaching fellowship programme among other activities.

TaLSS staff mostly have a professional or technical background, not academic. There are seven instructional designers who assist academics in putting their courses online.

ICT implementation strategy

For the first time in 2001 strategic planning was integrated with the budget process. QUT is a 'corporate' university with a large amount of central control over certain areas, eg branding and IT standards. There is some flexibility at the margins, but it has to be justified. The adoption of a virtual learning environment has been a top-down process.

With online teaching the primacy of academic control over content was a prime consideration. This was the justification for avoiding proprietory systems, such as Blackboard or WebCT, and opting instead for the in-house system, OLT. The intention was to set up a 'more flexible approach' based on what was most useful to academics.

The early adopters among the faculties, IT and Education, were given AUS$1m to work with the Business and Law faculties to get them using the new OLT system. As a managed learning environment OLT is 'more an idea and a support process'; a number of different tools are connected via a web framework. There is a course management database containing 800 modules underlying the OLT. The course management database is linked to the Library so that copyright clearance for online materials can be administered by the Library staff.

QUT has a partnership with Griffith University over database and licence agreements. The two universities also share students and have joined-up IT architecture and directory services to cross-authenticate staff and student access to each other's provision. QUT has a ratio of 1 PC to every 10 students.

Teaching and learning approaches

QUT's background as an Institute of Technology underpins a strong commitment to professional education. Courses and course planning are focussed on the industries and professions linked to the university. Face-to-face teaching is valued, as is the student experience on campus; there is a clear assumption that students will still want to study on campus, regardless of increasing online course provision.

The in-house virtual learning environment, OLT, has not changed the teaching paradigm at QUT. The instructional design model used was described as basically 'social constructivist', but whatever approach suits the discipline (i.e. whatever the academic in charge of the course chooses) is used. It appears that the OLT system itself has not been evaluated yet.

Staff development

Academic staff development

In the past QUT had a specialist unit for academic staff development, run by academics, but the unit was said to have 'developed its own research behaviour and lost its way'. Now they are focusing on an internal teaching fellowship scheme as the main route for staff development. The fellowships typically number between four to eight part-time secondments per semester, and the payment to the department is full salary plus on-costs (based on the ideas of the Derek Box Centre at Harvard).

The academic promotion scheme previously had four criteria: teaching, research, professional leadership and academic leadership. Following a review the promotion criteria were changed to: research and scholarship, teaching and the scholarship of teaching, and other leadership qualities. There is a performance development review but it is still not a requirement to show evidence of teaching evaluation.

It was reported that students ask why the academics don't have to have teaching qualifications, and one reason given was that the union is strongly opposed to teaching evaluation. There is a graduate certificate in higher education teaching but it is not mandatory and very few staff undertake it. This was previously delivered by the central unit but is now delivered by the education faculty. QUT has developed a framework of generic capabilities for staff, which at the time of our visit was still under discussion and had caused consternation.

The Online Teaching Steering Committee runs an annual conference to review developments in online teaching and raise awareness amongst staff. The 'Compassionate Pioneer Awards' are presented at this event; an idea taken from the AAHE in the USA. Compassionate Pioneers are defined as 'those who use (or support) new ways to improve teaching and learning AND who encourage and help their colleagues to do so'. The winners are only given a certificate, but this is still greatly appreciated. Students as well as staff can nominate potential recipients, who can be either academics or support staff.

Development for non-academic staff

During our visit we heard of a month-long, three-way job swap between the heads of IT Services, the Library and Teaching and Learning Support Services. The three Heads were holding weekly meetings to discuss issues, mostly concerning cultural differences between their departments. Neil Thelander (Head of IT Services, head-hunted by QUT to reform the department) described it as an action learning programme. The purpose was to provide opportunities for the senior managers to understand the constraints in the services (e.g. workload, or boundaries to the roles) in order to better integrate the three services. We noted that senior managers are all on five-year contracts and 360-degree feedback is used in their appraisal.

Casual staff (often overlooked in universities) now have access to facilities outside of their teaching hours and they are paid to attend training days.

Analysis and emerging themes

QUT is a booming place, proud of itself, and strongly established in the local marketplace. Whilst we heard it said that its 'position is stronger than its direction', QUT appears to be more determined than many institutions to made radical changes in the management and provision of courses to attract more students and from further afield. The senior management team is well aware of models for change (QUT was a major player in the 2000 DETYA study 'The business of borderless education'). Being a centralised and top-down institute, it is probably just a matter of time before the top administration gets inspired to gain a more international reputation.

Top-down change is bound to create animosity with some staff, and we became aware that some staff felt that their room for creativity had been restricted by the choice of an in-house learning environment (a retrograde move in at least one case).

In spite of the strong market focus, students are not much involved in decisions about online provision.

QUT Faculty of Education – examples of innovation

The QUT Education Faculty has 8,000 students, 5,000 fte. 50% are on campus, making it one of largest education faculties in Australia. The greatest provision of distance education at QUT is in the faculty of education.

The Faculty is running a Flexible Pedagogies Initiative until December 2002 (http://education.qut.edu.au/fo/fpi/fpihomebase.html). The initiative aims to explore and develop five different aspects of flexibility within the faculty, under the following project headings:

1. Complementary Approaches to Staff Development (CASE) – five levels of peer support (eg How do technologies help me work better?) and six technology activity areas (eg QUT systems) have been identified as relevant to the Faculty. A support site was set up, using a 'News' approach, to collect information about key technology areas such as induction activities, job requests and stories of good practice by peers.

2. Design of Media-enhanced Teaching (DOMET) – seven case studies are underway and are being shared using the News application developed for CASE. The integration of digital video in online teaching is a common theme.

3. Ubiquitous Network Integration in Teaching (UNIT) – exploring the use of a wireless network and laptops in one of the Faculty blocks, which featured an academic trial with 20 students in October 2001.

4. Media-enhanced Student Portfolios (MESP) – an evaluation of floppy disk cameras to help students capture video clips while undergoing training in the classroom. The video clips are embedded into the students' web sites for later analysis against the teaching attributes which they must acquire. The floppy disk cameras were found to be less complex to handle than other methods.

5. Student Satisfaction of Flexible Offerings (SSOFO) – conducting a review of the literature, QUT policies and recent projects on flexible learning and student satisfaction. An interim report has been published and a research methodology for 2002 agreed.

The Faculty has set up a web site called the Bridge to provide a one-stop-shop for advice (www.education.qut.edu.au/bridge/). Mini case studies of good practice are written up and put on the site. The staff are interviewed so they don't have to write the reports themselves.

In general, the Education faculty members feel that OLT does not serve their needs well. SMILE Advisers and instructional designers have never taught, and there appears to be a cultural gap between the academics and the 'young techies', who bring in characteristics of industry approaches to training which the education staff feel are not relevant to universities. The Education staff have to contact SMILE to get changes made to their OLT pages, which is felt to be very unsatisfactory. In response to this, in each of the 4 schools within the Faculty, people have volunteered to provide peer support to help their colleagues get online. The staff who offer this support are given some credit against their teaching hours in recognition of the time spent.

Recommended web-links

QUT IT services
www.its.qut.edu.au

QUT Online Teaching
http://olt.qut.edu.au

QUT Library
www.lib.qut.edu.au/elibrary/cmd/faqs.html

QUT Online Teaching Conference 2001
http://olt.qut.edu.au/int/olt2001

Staff capabilities
www.ala.org/acrl/ilstandardle.html

Student capabilities
http://cea.curtin.edu.au/ATN/

Flexible Pedagogies Initiative
http://education.qut.edu.au/fo/fpi/ fpihomebase.html

ATN Web site
www.atn.edu.au

6. Murdoch University

Wiebe Nijlunsing and Jill Armstrong

Context

Murdoch is a medium sized 'Sandstone university': a traditional university with a campus near a major town. Planning for Murdoch University began in 1970. The second university to be established in Western Australia and the seventeenth in Australia, it was constituted on 25 July 1973 by an Act of Parliament of Western Australia. In 1975, its inaugural year, Murdoch University enrolled 672 undergraduate students, had 6 Professors, a dynamic young staff and a Murdoch Campus of 254 hectares. Murdoch University has a second campus, the Rockingham Campus on Dixon Road, Rockingham. Today, Murdoch offers more than 50 undergraduate courses, has over 12,000 students enrolled and employs 1200 staff (570 academic staff and 770 general staff), including over 50 professorial staff. Murdoch University was named after Sir Walter Murdoch, a prominent Australian academic and essayist.

The only institution in Australia to have scored 5-stars for graduate satisfaction from the Good Universities Guide, for five years in a row, Murdoch has also been rated the best teaching campus of all Australia's public universities by an independent national survey of university graduates. This high standing was enhanced by two awards in the Prime Minister's 1998 Australian Awards for University Teaching. In 2001, in the Australian Awards for University Teaching, Professor Duane Varan won two out of seven prestigious national teaching awards. Murdoch University claims that it combines the best in university teaching with outstanding graduate satisfaction and a flexible outlook that lets students design the degree they need for their future.

Murdoch university mission is, 'To extend knowledge, stimulate learning, and promote understanding, for the benefit of the community.' In carrying out this mission Murdoch University aspires to be a world class university which is distinguished for excellence in teaching and research, accessibility, interdisciplinarity, and an international outlook. Of its student population of 12,000, about 80% are on undergraduate programmes, 10% doing higher degrees by taught programmes and 6% through research with nearly 4% on other post-graduate programmes and 0.45% on non-award bearing courses. In 2002 about 7500 are full-time, 3000 part-time and 1500 external students. Murdoch is organised into 4 divisions with a student load in 2000 in Business, Information Technology and Law of 39%, Science 18%, Social Sciences, Humanities and Education 37%, Veterinary and Biomedical Sciences 5%, and non-Divisional at 1%. Research Centres and Institutes (www.murdoch.edu.au/cwisindex/res) are also located in the Divisions.

Murdoch University is committed to international education and has developed important links with 73 institutions throughout the world. Of these, 33 are for the purposes of student exchange, 32 for academic and research collaboration and 8 for the teaching of Murdoch programs offshore. These links have contributed to an increasingly global outlook amongst its staff and students. The exchange partners are located in the English speaking countries and Asia. Murdoch is the national host for the Consortium for 'In-Country' Indonesian Studies (ACICIS www.sshe.murdoch.edu.au/acicis/).This is an Australian consortium of 17 universities, established by Murdoch, which arranges for Australian and International students to spend a semester or more studying at a limited number of

Indonesian partner universities. In 2001, a total of 2000 full-fee international students were enrolled at Murdoch.

e-Learning and the mission of the university

One of the few original Australian Universities to have involvement in distance learning (DL) Murdoch has recently reviewed its policy in the light of pressure on resources, wider DL provision and a national agenda of 'flexible learning' for widened participation. At its March 2002 meeting Murdoch Academic Council accepted the report of the Working Party on External Studies and Flexible Delivery and adopted its recommendations for a new approach to flexible teaching and learning. In brief this involves replacing the old delivery 'modes' - internal, external and online - with a new model of a unit in which the single coherent package of unit materials allow all students flexibility of access to the unit. The new unit package will consist of a reduced/streamlined print component, judicious use of complimentary online (with the potential to expand into a fuller use of online for those who wish it) and face-to-face sessions in which lectures are delivered in near real time to off campus students through various technologies.

The implications of such a shift are far-reaching and complex, but the proposed change is considered more cost effective (in terms of both time and resources), in keeping with trends in teaching and learning pedagogies, and is expected to enable the university to continue to deliver flexible learning to on and off campus students, despite increased resource constraints.

Learning and teaching approaches

Two types of provision for off campus studies are available: External Studies and Murdoch Online. For Murdoch Online, Internet access is essential, whereas for External Studies, unless specifically stated by a course, Internet access is not required, although it is a valuable, optional capability.

External studies

(www.oss.murdoch.edu.au/) External units consist of a core of specially written materials, including guides for self-paced study, supported where appropriate by audio and video cassette tapes, special audio-visual equipment, science kits, access to the Internet and, on some occasions, tele-conference sessions. Most of the units are designed for students who will study on their own without campus attendance. Some science units may however require attendance on campus.

Murdoch Online

(www.murdoch.edu.au/online/) is the University's coordinated approach to using the Internet for teaching and learning. 'Online' does not mean that all study activities are conducted online or 'on screen'. It means that for each unit Murdoch seeks to integrate the best combination of media and techniques, to match student needs and the nature of the subject area. Thus units taken online may utilise complementary resources and other forms of communication, for example textbooks, printed books of readings, telephone assistance, or in some cases on campus class attendance. Whilst many of the University's units of study utilise Internet-based resources, for example reference reading or email to tutors, Murdoch Online units are differentiated by having Internet-based delivery as an essential requirement. Murdoch Online units are in two main forms, aligned with the main kinds of circumstances for their students. These are:

Online external–campus attendance not required

Online internal–integrated with weekly classes.

Murdoch Online units are based on a core of specially-prepared web pages, typically structured into a study guide section, detailing how the unit is organised, a topics section which presents study materials, learning activities and online references from the Internet, and sections for technical help, tutor contacts, class discussion groups and assignments. Nearly all units are based upon the WebCT environment, with supporting resources from other media and services, especially textbooks and telephone or classroom availability of tutors.

Implementation strategy

The introduction of WebCT has been the catalyst for the introduction of a new student record system, Callista. Use of Callista has resulted in stabilising student processes, by creating a usable method of online registration for students and reducing re-enrolment into new modules by 50%. Examples of the use of WebCT were presented. One of the more interesting uses is that by the library who have set up a literacy foundation programme for students on WebCT. It is called the Library and Information Technology Exercise (LITE) programme and can be found at www.lib.murdoch.edu.au/lite.

The Teaching and Learning Centre (cleo.murdoch.edu.au/tlc/) led by Rick Cummings works with both staff and student development and has been in existence over three years, but grew from a centre supporting distance education. A student service team focuses on helping students develop learning skills and a staff service team focuses on helping staff develop online skills. The Centre offers support for educational design skills. It helps evaluate teaching courses. The Centre also runs the qualification for HE lecturers at Murdoch.

Library

Murdoch University Library (www.lib.murdoch.edu.au/) provides a focus point for university life and studies. The Library's collection of more than 570,000 print items is housed in the Murdoch Campus Library, the Veterinary Branch Library and the Rockingham Regional Campus Community Library. The Library provides access to a wide range of information in electronic form at all sites. Much of this information, including access to the catalogues of other university libraries, is also available from home for students who have a modem and access to the University's network. The rapid growth in electronic information means that library users need to be able to retrieve and manipulate electronic texts. The Library has an extensive programme of education and training to ensure that everyone is able to use its services effectively.

There is collaboration between Western Australia libraries. This was set up a number of years ago and there is a joint project to find an acceptable authentication scheme for wider HE use. At Murdoch in 2001 the access management system used 'passwords' for login to the systems and services were synchronised with Student PINs held in the MAIS database. Since then, synchronisation of PIN/Password has become available for some systems and services. Internet Traffic & Modem Time Quota System is used to manage Student Internet Quota, MAIS is used to authenticate users before allowing them to access restricted information resources and services e.g. the Library's Electronic Reserve, Exam Papers, MyInfo The Web interface to the Student Information System (Callista) and WebCT, are used to manage unit materials online.

Analysis and emerging issues

Murdoch is a medium sized university that takes a systematic approach to using ICT in an effective way. Pressure on reduced unit resource and competition for students that face all Australian universities has led to consideration of a potentially radical shift in its approach to course organisation. The past distinction between external and internal courses and the ways these are offered is to be amalgamated in a new 'flexible' approach and there appears to be a commitment to real process engineering to enable this. The emphasis is shifting from delivery to access, underwritten by questions of how students will become responsible for their own learning, and grow their motivation to succeed. Murdoch University seeks to gain a more flexible infrastructure using web-technologies to underpin this development. There will be a five-year implementation process and which progressively moves units into flexible mode. It is recognised that a change in culture needs to happen.

Specific case description

The ASCILITE CUTSD Evaluation project led by Rob Phillips takes a new approach to the evaluation of the impact of using ICT in higher education. The project was aimed at developing a framework for helping academic and research staff design suitable evaluation processes for ICT projects. The evaluation research is concerned with the learning environment, learning process, and learning outcomes. This project was inspired by the outcomes of the Shirley Alexander report that highlighted that most ICT projects were not

properly designed and/or evaluated. The project has been completed and a Learner Centred Evaluation framework (LCE) was developed. An evaluation framework has been developed for use in the projects and is downloadable from: cleo.murdoch.edu.au/projects/cutsd99/.

7. Edith Cowan University: How to make quality strategies and business strategies meet

Bas Cordewener and Arthur Loughran

Context

Edith Cowan University (ECU) has over 20,000 students and about 3,000 are distance education students. ECU has emerged out of about 5 educational institutes, including teacher colleges and an academy for arts. This has led to a lot of interest in different educational approaches in which the available technology and multi-media play an important role.

Edith Cowan University is not the only Perth-based University. Competition exists with the University of Western Australia (UWA), Murdoch University, Curtin University and Notre Dame University. To ensure future existence a healthy inflow of students is required. To attract this inflow ECU chose a profile in which the university "seeks to become the leader in the education of learners for the knowledge-based services and professions". To achieve this goal, three themes have been identified to pursue:

1. Service (adopting a student-centred approach in learning and administration and close involvement with stakeholders and the community).

2. Professionalism (produce graduates that satisfy industrial demand and community in skills and behaviour).

3. Enterprise (growth, commercially sound, international prestige).

e-Learning and the mission of the university

From the very beginning the university took a lot of interest in digital education and multimedia, having the technology for distance learning available. Now the Centre for Research and Information Technology and Communication (CRITC) has a focal role within the university by

conducting acclaimed research in the field of learning, advising the board and supporting professional development of staff. The head of CRITC, Professor Ron Oliver, is from the School of Communication And Multimedia (SCAM), which develops and uses innovative applications. Authentic learning, Self-regulated learning and Communities of Practice are research topics. It is acknowledged that the work and ideas of CRITC have a strong influence on the institutional view of e-learning. On the other hand it is still possible that in other parts of the university a lot of energy will be invested in duplicating this work unknowingly.

Research is not the only driver for the interest in e-learning. ECU is trying to secure its existence and it is thought that e-learning activities will improve the chances for the university to prosper and generate additional income.

The main reasons for ECU to seriously address e-learning are:

- a 50% cut down in government funding;

- the political pressure (aren't there too many universities in Western Australia?);

- the availability of lucrative Asian student markets.

In fact ECU is engaged in an extensive outreach to Australian and foreign students as it tries to ensure economic viability for the coming years. It does so with a clear philosophy to provide quality education.

e-Learning philosophy

Edith Cowan wishes to provide higher education of a high quality level to as many national and international students as possible. This is backed up by the notion that ECU's primary task is to supply graduates that are professionals possessing the skills that industry needs and wants. Investment in innovative education through the use of IT should provide the means for the delivery of distance education courses that meet the principles that ECU believes to be crucial: flexibility, relevance, currency, cultural inclusivity, and a concern for the needs of the learner.

To deliver education for skilled professionals ECU is using IT to reform its curriculum. This is done by offering high quality interactive educational processes that sustain the constructivist pedagogical concept. The close relations between the researchers (CRITC), the decision-makers (committees, academic board) and having IT-capable faculty within the School for Communication and Multimedia to try out the implementation of new education, has a powerful impact on the adoption of new educational concepts by the ECU. In these new ways of developing and delivering online education the need for compatible technologies and for metadata to describe learning materials has also led to awareness of standards like EDNA (EDNA is the Australian adaptation of Dublin Core/IMS specifications).

Though this is very encouraging it must be noted that the CRITC research team is quite a large group of enthusiasts that to a certain extent can pursue their own interests, which are not limited by the current capabilities of staff and technology, nor directly tied to university resources. There may be problems as the university as a whole is required to follow the proposed educational changes in the coming years.

Examples of CRITC research and design

Joe Luca, a lecturer at ECU, offers the Project Management Methodology course, an example of a simulated web environment in which students perform authentic Project Management (PM) tasks. After negotiating about their role in a PM assignment, they perform the tasks belonging to it. The assessment is done in three ways:

1. A self-evaluation (publicly).

2. A peer review of the others (only known to the teacher).

3. An assessment meeting, where the group discusses the self-assessments.

Both students and teachers are highly motivated by this situation, because of the realistic feel and the very tangible role aspects. Now that the custom application has been developed it may be possible to build a similar, but generic, model in a virtual learning environment like Blackboard. The reviews will eventually lead to a digital portfolio (DPF) system, so the student can control and use the DPF as a guide for reflection, study planning and to support applications for future employment. This kind of project makes the institute aware of the potential benefits and drawbacks of a standard digital portfolio. There has not yet been a decision on the adoption of a standard DPF for ECU, or how to get it: proprietary software or in-house development.

Chris Brooke (PhD student) does research on the principles for the design of communities of practice. He finds encouragement in community psychology, which suggests the need for a clear purpose if such communities are to persist over time. Jen Herrington (researcher) advocates the principle of authentic learning as distinct from the usual practice which tends to overemphasise availability of information. The information focus leads to 'canned' content and assessment focussed on the packaged content, which is not an authentic situation. What seems authentic for the teacher may not be authentic for the student. Mark MacMahon researches on self-regulated learning.

Learning Development Services (LDS)

By establishing the Learning Development Services centre (LDS), which has a budget that faculty may use for resource and staff development, ECU initiated an institutional program for professional resource and staff development. The budget may be used if the proposed changes in education fit into the university strategy. The goals of LDS are described in the ECU Online Framework, which can be used as a checklist for critical elements of effective learning environments. The list contains items addressing pedagogical, resource and delivery issues. Overall conditions that must be met in order for proposed educational developments to qualify for support are: Quality Assurance and Extra Revenues. Quality Assurance means that proposals for innovative change must show how the quality of education will increase as a result of the changes; the Extra Revenues condition means that the proposed innovation should have a positive impact either by conquering new markets or by a more efficient delivery of education.

This may seem an excessively commercial approach, but ECU has learned from its past. A few years ago there was no sustainable system for calculating the costs, let alone a system based upon a business model and ECU had a hard time when the federal government cut heavily on funding. In a competitive HE-system a strict business plan is essential as well as a process of assessing the returns of an investment in innovation.

LDS support on a Service Level Agreement (SLA) basis

A survey of the available online education established a starting position, which was consolidated into a database that is maintained to look carefully at the progress made. As well as compulsory courses for teachers (assigned by the Head of School) the LDS uses grants to set resource and staff development in motion to increase the online supply. This will be supported by 'lighthouse' staff, technicians specially qualified to advise on setting up inspiring Blackboard courses. The LDS has worked out a comprehensive model of the working structure for resource and professional development. Collaboration between faculty and LDS is negotiated and formulated in a Service Level Agreement (SLA). The SLA describes what workshops will be set up and what modules will be upgraded to mode A (web supplemental), mode B (web dependent) or mode C (fully online) A lot of effort is now put in mode B: the introduction of Blackboard (20 February 2002) has built up speed and has an enormous impact on the demand for Professional Development to use this virtual learning environment well. An effort will be made to attract more high-level staff for the workshops and focus in on aspects of quality and strategy. To be qualified as being C mode is difficult because in most cases online assessment is not really available. LDS is working on the design of a digital portfolio. If that becomes available it may help the certification of innovational units, which can then be recognised as fully online education.

The activities of LDS seem to have had positive results and have met with enthusiasm. The approach of the current development program represents a traditional method: experts telling target groups what they need to do. The 'Alverno (Milwaukee) experience' however, has inspired a strand of thinking which is trying to differentiate the development services on a faculty basis. It is hoped that this will better anticipate specific needs and offer training on salient issues in an authentic context. This will also offer a better opportunity to certify the mode B and C units (modules). This distinct approach will be launched by appointing LDS account managers to divisions of faculties. The question of whether this will exclude cross-fertilisation between different faculties remains unanswered.

Collaborative student and library services

A lot of effort is put into student services, which of course are important to high quality delivery of distance education. A student portal has been designed and built, in collaboration with students, mainly to enable communication and information exchange. Online enrolment in the new Callista database (collaboratively with other Western Australian universities) has almost been accomplished.

The ECU library doesn't have a strong position, nor is its role in digital education seen as important. They were not included in the LDS Online working structure and are not seen as a target group for the PD program. This is in contradiction with the trend that libraries are growing in importance in the field of resource and knowledge management, procuring learning materials and information quality assurance.

The ECU library participates in an Australian National Training Authority funded project (ANTA) that is aimed at online materials development. All the libraries of Western Australia give admission to all resources to students of other Western Australian universities, a direct response to the economic climate (the Australian dollar lost a third of its worth against the US dollar). To keep online resources available the Western Australian university libraries had only one option: to share. Another remarkable collaboration exists between Griffith University and ECU: registered Blackboard trainers from Griffith came to ECU and ECU helped Griffith with technical issues by sending their 'lighthouse-staff'.

Analysis and emerging themes

Edith Cowan is a university that really has a keen eye on modern education and strives to use the possibilities of online teaching and learning from a research or quality perspective as well as from a organisational and company perspective. In its development, implementation and staff development ECU is very seriously and consciously working according to strict rules. ECU may face a possible conflict between the interests of the business strategy and the quality strategy. Strictly planned professional development activities are not always the most effective ones; commercial attractiveness and expensive educational requirements can be opposed to one another. Policy decisions on that level are made at the highest management level of ECU. Though the Dutch/British visitors cannot predict the future we feel that ECU is well placed to continue providing a high quality university education.

Recommended web-links

Information about Edith Cowan University can be found on the following web-links:

Edith Cowan University
www.cowan.edu.au/

ECU, further and higher education
http://cofhe.www.ecu.edu.au/index.html

ECU, technologies
www.ecu.edu.au/lift/

ECU, student
http://student.ecu.edu.au/VC/

8. The University of Southern Queensland, Toowoomba
'It is better to create the future than to predict it'[1]

Annette Roeters and Helen McEvoy

Context

Originally founded as a College of Advanced Education in 1967, the University of Southern Queensland (USQ) has been involved in distance education since 1977 when it commenced implementing dual-mode programmes. In 1989, the college achieved university status with the formal founding of the University of Southern Queensland. The Australian Federal Government designated USQ a National Distance Education Centre. Students are enrolled on a variety of programmes. The actual numbers for 2001 comprised 5266 on campus students and nearly 16,000 external students (75%) from over 60 countries. Forty-five of those countries have access to USQ's online learning facilities and all are mixed-mode (print, CDs, audio). In 2001, the total staff numbers comprised 1,302 with 536 representing academic members. A Regional Liaison Officer network of part-time staff are employed down the Eastern Seaboard of Australia to provide local support to distance learners.

As expected from its origins, the USQ has a strong foundation in the provision of education courses, both at undergraduate and postgraduate levels. Additionally, it has established four other faculties across the Arts, Business and Commerce, Engineering and Surveying and the Sciences providing courses in areas such as accounting, information technology, health communication, nursing and accounting.

A major focus of USQ is to continue to be a leader in international and distance education. Professor Peter Swannell, the Vice-Chancellor of the University has stated that 'the important characteristic of a successful e-University is that it surrounds its people with the best possible technology, implementing the best possible pedagogy' (Swannell 2002). He states that people are of central importance to the educational process supported by the use of high quality, carefully designed and delivered study materials. The USQ is proud of its reputation as an international leader in online and distance learning aiming to provide flexible study choice to students through on campus, off campus and online options. Recently, the USQ was named joint winner of the Good Universities Guides, Australia's University of the Year for 2000-2001. The award was achieved for excellence in developing the e-university.

e-Learning and the mission of the university

Senior managers of the USQ have a strong vision of the placement of this university within both the global and the Australian higher education sectors. Professor James Taylor states that their objective is to be 'fast, flexible and fluid', enabling the USQ to respond to the e-challenge of continuous, dynamic change. The USQ presents an example of a university that has strategically committed to, and heavily invested in, Internet and Web-based distance education provision. A financial opportunity provided by a Federal Government grant, has enabled the university to develop the technical infrastructure to take USQ into the fifth generation of distance education (e-University).

1 Professor James Taylor

The e-University

Professor James Taylor suggests that a fifth generation of distance learning is emerging. The fifth generation is essentially a derivation of the fourth generation, taking further advantage of features of the Internet and the Web. Taylor calls this new generation the 'Intelligent Flexible Learning Model'. Taylor's five generations are:

1. The Correspondence Model – print based.

2. The Multi-media Model – print, audio and video technologies utilised.

3. The Telelearning Model – based on applications of telecommunication technologies (allows synchronous communication) – interactive.

4. The Flexible Learning Model – based on access delivery via the Internet and Web.

5. The Intelligent Flexible Learning Model – involving further exploitation of new technologies.

Taylor suggests 'fifth generation distance education has the potential to decrease significantly the costs associated with providing access to institutional processes and online tuition.' (Taylor 2001) He proposes that the fifth generation model is suitably illustrated by the USQ's e-University Project and its focus on three fundamental areas:

- the e-Information repositories;
- a variety of e-Applications;
- and the e-Interface respectively.

www.usq.edu.au/electpub/e-jist/docs/old/vol4no1/2001docs/taylor.html

A graphic overview of USQ's e-University Project is presented in Figure 4.

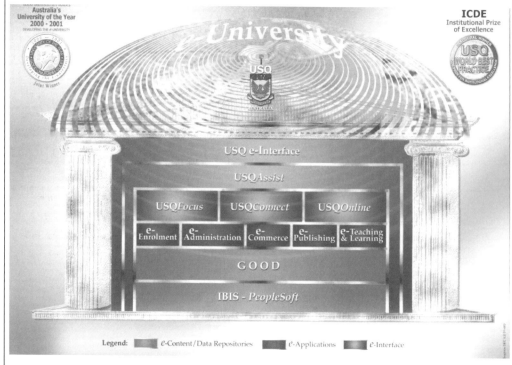

Figure 4: The e-University Project

Professor Taylor discussed USQAssist (an automated, online customer service/relations management project) as a disintermediation example that epitomises the concept of the fifth generation model. The automated project builds on previous knowledge creating an increasingly populated database of answers to common queries.

The intelligent flexible learning model is predicted on interactive multimedia online, Internet-based access to World Wide Web resources, automated response systems, and portals to administrative and reading resources. Taylor's model would automate most interaction between student and teacher/institution, thus reducing the variable costs associated with increasing student numbers, whether on or off campus. A tenfold productivity increase will be achieved from student tutor ratios of 20:1 to 200:1, producing a 'quantum leap in economies of scale and associated cost-effectiveness.' (Taylor 2001)

In 1996/7, under the leadership of the Vice-Chancellor, Professor Peter Swannell, the USQ made the decision to place itself at the forefront of online delivery. The decision was taken to develop fully online courses primarily in postgraduate course areas. USQOnline was conceived as a separate platform to present online teaching and learning.

In a unique partnership arrangement for a higher education institution, the USQ bought a 25% stake in the Hong Kong based company NextEd to supply online services to fee-paying online learners primarily throughout the Asian and Middle Eastern market sectors. The USQ's stake in NextEd was reduced to 11.3% in 2000 but it continues to be a major client. Effectively, NextEd works directly with USQ as a partner to USQOnline to provide server coverage to offshore students; providing mirror sites on a global scale, a technical helpdesk, and marketing services.

Distance Education Centre (DEC)

The role played by the DEC has been fundamental to the implementation of the USQ's e-learning strategy. The DEC staff of 125 is centrally involved in the design, development and delivery of study packages to online and distance learners. Through an integrated team of instructional designers, media specialists, multimedia experts, electronic publishing staff, graphic artists, photographers, network services, distribution services and student support staff in the DEC, USQ has aimed to create a total course materials preparation centre.

A team of nine academic instructional designers work closely with academics from all faculty areas to ensure that course materials are of an appropriate standard and purpose. In an attempt to gain improvements in efficiency, USQ is in the process of developing new course development and production systems. Academics will have increased flexibility to create online and distance packages using DEC specialist staff for instructional and design advice, for multi-media expertise, for copyright clearance and for proof reading.

DEC is more than a 'production house' for the development of learning materials. It undertakes research and evaluation activities, has its own research plan and conducts a regular workshop/seminar series for staff. It also produces its own international, peer-reviewed journal, e-JIST (Electronic Journal of Instructional Science and Technology www.usq.edu.au/electpub/e-jist/).

Implementation strategies

Central to the implementation of the USQ's corporate strategy, is a top down transformation of the educative culture of the university, using state of the art technology to create an enabling infrastructure.

Key issues in implementation are:

- Incremental integration of business processes through the introduction of a new administrative system from PeopleSoft.

- Simultaneously building commercial partnerships (NextEd) while developing home controlled alternatives to achieve interoperability.

- The development of campus-wide wireless technology.

- Plans to develop a webSlate device to facilitate teaching and learning and online campus access through the use of wireless technology.

- Employment of new staff prepared to be open to a culture of change.

- Workshops for writers and developers of distance learning materials to assist in the development and updating of online courses.

- Federal Government injection of cash to support the concept of an e-University.

USQOnline - Initially, USQOnline has been launched on the NextEd platform.

Programmes are available across all faculties. Some 32 full programmes are available through USQOnline involving some 160 separate courses. To achieve interoperability, USQ is also revamping its undergraduate online platform using WebCT in 2002.

PeopleSoft – In 1999 a decision was taken to update USQ's administrative systems. Financial and human resource management systems are already online, and student administration is due to come online in May 2002. At considerable cost, this significant investment for the university helps provide an efficient and effective basis for the development of e-learning and teaching and a step closer to the fully integrated managed learning environment.

As part of existing commercial arrangements, NextEd provides USQ with Blackboard software and servers. While Professor Taylor says that the relationship with NextEd is 'going quite well at the moment', the University's business model is to work directly with the customer, eliminating the need for the intermediary group (disintermediation). To achieve interoperability, the USQ is looking at providing its own marketing services and expanding its own online platform using WebCT.

Teaching and learning approaches

'Teaching and learning drives things, not the software' (Associate Professor Glen Postle)

USQ has taken a focussed corporate approach to the provision of flexible learning through maximising the choice of programmes available – on campus, off campus and online.

Unit team approach

Refers to the generation of distance and online teaching packages through the creative use of multi-disciplinary teams using a 'generator model'.

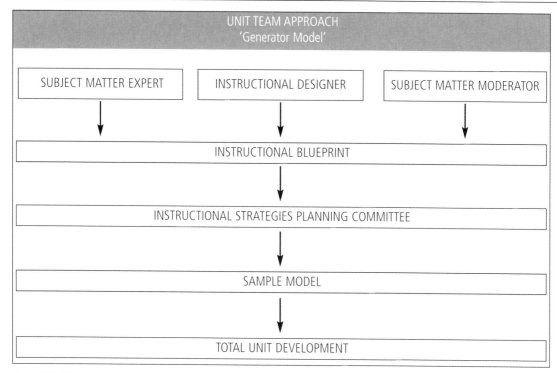

Figure 5: Unit Team Approach

Group models

Central to the philosophy of online teaching and learning at USQ is what is described as 'the creation of communities of practice' (Professor James Taylor). The rationale is to create the 'collaborative, reflective practitioner' through the intelligent use of online group work facilitated by an online tutor. The pedagogical approach is constructivist, which involves students interacting with each other and working on real work problems (with explicit rules of engagement for both students and staff).

In terms of monitoring how well online learning is functioning, and for the concept of 'a pedagogy of community of performance' to be successful, it is essential to understand how group members are working. Professor James Taylor has suggested that there are three major

patterns of performance. The first two categories, workers and lurkers while operating in different ways, do participate equally. The third category, sleepers do not seem to be engaging with the group learning process.

USQ is constantly analysing the performance of students in online group work through analysis of online 'hits' per student. These statistics are automatically generated by the NextEd system. Data is available to show usage against time of day, day of the week, and across months of the year. The results of the analysis are to be used to allow better support systems to be put in place. Recent analysis showed usage was predominantly focused on discussion and communication between lecturer/facilitator and learners, with content areas next most frequently accessed, followed by learner to learner group or individual communication.

Library

The library exists to enhance and assist the teaching and learning process, and library policy attempts to provide equity of service to all users whether on campus or off campus. The situation as regards online users is more complicated as online packages are designed to be self-help facilities. In theory, an online student should not require the services of the library to directly support their learning although any extra reading around a subject can enhance the learning process.

Off campus library services are designed to mirror on campus services through the provision of:

- a reference enquiry service for off campus users;

- posting photocopies of journal articles;

- postal loan service of monographs;

- audio visual postal loan service;

- online tutorials in the use of e-resources.

In an effort to be as accessible as possible, staff respond to enquiries sent by post, fax or via the World Wide Web. The library also supplies a freecall number if readers prefer to contact them directly. The off campus library service is available to externally enrolled USQ students who live in Australia and more than 50 kilometres from Toowoomba. A restricted service is also available to external students living overseas.

Library service provision is clearly about attempting to bring library services to all registered USQ users. Central to this vision is the provision of electronic resources (e-resources) to all registered users.

The library policy encompasses:

- the retention of budget control by the library – purchasing power is not devolved to the faculties but the university library consults with academic staff on spending priorities;

- the use of academic liaison librarians to create active partnerships with academic areas – academic liaison librarians spend part of each working day in the academic department;

- working on some multidisciplinary development teams to determine policy and direction;

- working with educational developers to ensure accuracy of library details in any course material;

- the library is part of the accreditation process of any new course – this ensures that the library has adequate foreknowledge to ensure supply and availability of course material;

- hands-on user education sessions for on campus users and online tutorials for off campus students;

The library would like to move into an integrated web environment with more seamless access to library services from other interfaces. It has proved difficult to do this. With three-quarters of USQ students off campus, the university gives prominence to developing and maintaining the USQ portal. Licensing of electronic resources is an ongoing problem. Many suppliers will not allow remote access so the library has a policy of only taking resources that do allow off campus use. There is one exception and that is the database supplying Australian census material. The library's response is to undertake searches of this particular database for any student who requires it.

Analysis and emerging issues

The USQ is responding to the many challenges arising from offering quality on campus as well as off campus teaching and learning. The USQ's early involvement in the Australian Universities Quality Audit has prompted a major review of assessment procedures and moves towards increased consistency of approach across the whole institution. The overall USQ approach is pragmatic ('we have to do it or face the prospect of disappearing') and highly focused, primarily resting with off-shore/external students, especially on online students.

The vision of a corporate university is strongly led by those at the senior management level but also strongly supported by faculties and other university cost centres. However, as the USQ works to transform its vision into reality, it does seem to be strongly reliant on the continuing presence of a few key members of senior staff. Technically, the strategic vision is to invest in university-wide systems. One such system, the installation of campus-wide wireless technology, is proceeding in the technology to enable on campus students to utilise it. It would seem that staff are going to be the primary beneficiaries of this technology.

The various e-University projects and the resulting commitment to the development and implementation of automated courseware production systems (with e-content management systems enabling cross-media publication from a single stored source), online teaching and learning, automated pedagogical advice systems, and automated business systems, are still in the transition phase from concept to reality. The on campus student also benefits indirectly from these innovations, with flexible programmes being attractive to students who want to do just one or two courses/subjects/units and those who already have full-time or part-time work commitments.

NextEd as a commercial partner. NextEd customised Blackboard for USQ. To improve independence the USQ also bought WebCT – running two separate systems to enhance interoperability might be an expensive solution.

As only 10% of potential library users take up distance services, the library needs to examine firstly its marketing strategy and secondly the range of services it supplies.

References

Swannell, P., (2002). 2002 Distance education student guide. Toowoomba: DEC, USQ.

Taylor, J.C., (2001). Automating e-learning: the future of higher education. The International conference on emerging telecommunications applications (ICETA) Kosice, Slovakia, 17-19 October, 2001.

Recommended web-links

University of Southern Queensland homepage
www.usq.edu.au/

USQ Online
www.usqonline.com.au/

USQ Connect
www.usq.edu.au/usqconnect/brochure/
index.html

DEC – Distance Education Centre
www.usq.edu.au/dec/

USQ Library Services
www.usq.edu.au/library/

Fifth Generation Distance Learning. Article by
Professor Jim Taylor
www.usq.edu.au/electpub/ejist/docs/
old/vol4no1/2001docs/pdf/Taylor.pdf

Virtual Education Institutions in Australia:
Between the idea and the Reality. A chapter
co-written by Suellen Tapsall and Dr. Yoni Ryan
www.col.org/virtualed/chapter10.pdf

Teaching Online: Challenge to a reinterpretation
of Traditional Instructional Models. A paper
co-written by Jacquie McDonald and Glen Postle
http://ausweb.scu.edu.au/aw99/papers/
mcdonald/paper.htm

9. Griffith University: Adapting to flexible learning

Marcel Mirande and Rhonda Riachi

Context

Griffith University, Brisbane, founded in 1975, is now a six-campus university with approximately 24,000 students and 2,800 staff. As well as its original and largest Nathan location, the University has five other campuses including:

- Mt Gravatt – education faculty, teacher training.

- Gold Coast – growing fast, will be largest.

- Logan – new campus added later (1998) with a focus on student-centred learning and high-tech profile.

- Southbank – the Queensland Conservatorium.

- Southbank – the Queensland College of Art.

All campuses attract up to 85% local students, most commute and 3,000 students from over 70 countries travel to Griffith to complete one of the 690 courses on offer to overseas students. A wide range of degrees is offered, from biomedical science to international business, aviation to education, law to music, engineering to fine art, IT to psychology, the environment to the humanities, laser sciences to languages, and nursing to physiotherapy, to name just a few.

University approach to e-Learning

The philosophy behind Griffith's approach to higher education is captured in its mission statement: "Griffith University is committed to innovation, bringing disciplines together, internationalisation, equity and justice (and) lifelong learning for the enrichment of Queensland, Australia and the international community". Griffith values 'flexible learning' as a means of enhancing learning and providing the richest learning experience for all students.

Flexible learning at Griffith is an educational approach using a variety of student-centred teaching and learning methods, resources and flexible administrative practices that respond to the needs of a diverse student population. Flexible learning practices are designed to increase:

- flexibility of participation and access;

- flexibility of progression and assessment;

- flexibility with regard to learner control and choice;

- appropriate use of a range of learning technologies and resources;

- learner support and access to information and services;

- commitment to academic excellence.

A major thrust of flexible learning at Griffith is the use of the Web to support teaching and learning. As part of this thrust, all degree programmes and courses offered in flexible mode include some form of Web presence to support student learning. The level of presence will vary according to a range of factors but may see a subject being:

- Web-based – where the course is dependent on the content and activities on the web site;

- Web-enhanced – which improves the learning experience by enrichment and interaction in a way not available through other resources;

- Web-supported – where the Web site plays a significant role in the course by providing an alternative means of accessing learning materials.

Support for teaching and learning

The Griffith Institute for Higher Education (GIHE) is the University's academic staff development unit and has developed a series of print resources (Teaching Through Flexible Learning), an online discussion forum, and courses and workshops to assist academic staff to conceptualise online contributions to good university teaching. GIHE is centrally funded, as is the Flexible Learning and Access Services (FLAS) unit, which provides educational design facilities and additional support for academic staff. FLAS developed the ADAPT program (Academic Development and Professional Training Program) to assist academic staff in the design and development of flexible learning resources within the Blackboard teaching and learning environment. The aim of the ADAPT program includes the following areas:

- Planning for flexible and student centred learning.

- Managing flexible and student centred learning.

- Better resource preparation for flexible and student-centred learning.

- Better teaching for flexible and student centred learning.

ADAPT organises courses into a framework based on different levels:

- Level 1: 'survival' - enables quick access to design and technical tips.

- Level 2: 'consolidating and enhancing practice' - gives in-depth information about flexible learning design.

- Level 3: 'exploring and experimenting' - provides a forum for peer discussion on flexible learning design issues.

As the programme is intended to be an integrated model that embraces all stages of teaching in an online environment, it is also divided into several phases, which represent the process of planning, preparing, developing, delivering and evaluating online education.

Each year there are calls for expressions of interest for conversion of courses to flexible learning delivery and then support is allocated. The Pro Vice-Chancellor and Deans make proposals, and the Deputy Vice-Chancellor (Teaching and Learning) decides which courses get funding. Team-work takes place with academics, graphic designers, etc, for multimedia and print distribution.

Implementation strategy

The Logan Campus was the first to try flexible learning in a corporate way, with the intention of extending this to other campuses. The former Vice-Chancellor decided that Logan should be the launch site for 'flexible learning'. There were several reasons to start with flexible learning, including 'you can't not do it'; innovation; new markets; and the need to equip students with skills for work. Griffith started the Logan campus in 1998. It was purpose-built, planned and funded by the Federal and State Governments as a high-tech campus for a high unemployment area. The campus has 200 staff, of which 50 are academic, and 100 teachers are from other campuses.

The campus started with a group of self-selected teachers, who were enthusiastic to do something new: less face-to-face lecturing and more independent learning, with a high level of support (about half of the 50 support staff worked in Logan during the first phase). Every subject had to have a Web site. There was a ratio of 1 computer to 4 students as well as a

Microwave link, and a high-speed, wideband network. However, the experiment in independent learning went too far for some students – e.g. there was only one meeting with the tutor per week for first-year students in some courses. Some students had difficulties with the tutors' emphasis on teamwork as a primary part of 'flexible learning'. Student retention was a concern. As a consequence, some traditional methods were reinstated and a greater emphasis was put on choice. A formal orientation programme for students was introduced to prepare them to adjust from a high school environment to the more open university environment where there was more choice and a greater responsibility for their own learning.

There were many difficulties with IT in the early days. Griffith introduced Blackboard in 2001, which improved maintenance of Web sites, as it enabled teaching staff to update and maintain the sites (the old system was controlled via webmasters). Frustrations with the old system had led to some schools setting up their own sites outside the system. Blackboard was introduced in part from a recognition that the central support system could not be sustained, and that individual staff needed to have responsibility for their own course developments. Now the staff work on common templates for courses and academics have more control of the content. The university is trying to develop a consistent front-end on all course Web sites.

'Logan Campus: What have we learned? 1998-2001' is a detailed in-house report by Peter Taylor and Jason Blaik (published after a local symposium in 2001). The Executive Summary of this report (pp. 4-10) praised "the strong campus leadership, significant resource allocations (including the IT infrastructure), the purpose-built learning environments" as well as "the

enthusiasm of the dedicated staff". The introduction of flexible learning was seen "in the short to medium term" to have changed "the roles and workloads of both staff and students", with both positive and negative implications. Some staff wanted their curriculum and web-development work to be given greater recognition by their School/Department so that their achievements could contribute to their staff appraisals. One positive consequence of this environment was the launching of the national project for the Peer Review of ICT Teaching Resources – a structured process through which academics could gain reward and recognition of their scholarship in the area of teaching (www.peerreview.com.au).

Support services for student learning were embedded in many courses offered at Logan. Whilst the library and Learning Assistance Unit (LAU) offered workshops, staff sought to embed these workshops into discipline-specific contexts – almost on a 'just-in-time' basis (e.g. workshop on assignment writing before assignments were due). The general staff at Logan provided important support in the context of reduced academic contact time.

The 'Logan Campus: What have we learned?' report concluded that, while students experienced some difficulty in gaining access to academic staff, "student academic achievements in this flexible learning environment have been impressive". However, sustaining "what has been achieved...(will be) a challenge".

Teaching and learning approaches

Student induction and orientation at Logan plays an important role. There are two entry routes into Logan, traditional HE entry plus another route where students are interviewed up to a year in advance and are gradually prepared for the Logan experience. They are given an access course before starting and all students then have a quite intensive Week 0 induction.

Griffith has an interesting concept of learning centres: a cluster of teaching facilities with a central room, breakout rooms and computer rooms. There is a serious attempt to use space differently, e.g. students are given a problem and then move to breakout rooms to solve it. The Logan buildings have been modified slightly since built (e.g. needed to go via one room to get to another) and are not used strictly as intended. One new building on Logan has no learning centres but has more flexible rooms and bigger spaces. These spaces are used most innovatively by the BA course in Human Services, which holds weekly meetings ('common time') of staff and students with a different theme each time (e.g. essay-writing skills). These meetings achieve 80% attendance and have been running for 3 years in response to students' concerns that there was 'not enough access to staff'.

Learning@GU is the student/staff portal. Students log into the Blackboard portal that is part of a wider enterprise system linking all student information databases, learning resources and tools together to achieve a more student-centred environment.

Staff development

Griffith has provided small-group-based workshops on the principles of flexible learning, focusing on the design of effective pedagogies to achieve individual and group learning outcomes consistent with the aims of programmes and their constituent courses. These workshops are not aimed specifically towards any particular software product. GIHE and FLAS have also offered jointly a Graduate Certificate in Flexible Learning.

The ADAPT staff development courses run by FLAS are available online in conjunction with workshops. The workshops are based on small groups in the same schools. Courses are set up to allow individual staff to dip in and use when they have a specific need. Griffith offers this staff development partly to help cognate groups work together.

According to Janice Rickards, Pro Vice-Chancellor, staff development and cultural change are the most important issues when moving to flexible learning. Both are still underway and have proved expensive and difficult, as intensive staff development has been needed. Changes are stimulated by the supply of funding to academic schools to move courses online. Priorities for 2002 include multi-campus courses and completing efforts to put whole programmes online. One University priority is to develop flexible courses and full programmes that can be across all campuses. Sharing and re-use within schools is on the agenda – funding is available to get schools to develop one course to replace multiple iterations of the same topic.

Relationships

There is a variety of relationships with industry and government. Perhaps the most obvious has been the funding of the capital works (buildings) at the Logan Campus, via state and national government funding.

The Logan Campus has also attracted other external funds. Sun Microsystems donated AU$220,000 to have its name attached to a major computer-work room and a private-enterprise donation has funded graduate student accommodation on the campus (AU$6 million already and AU$6 million more to come). The School of Human Services has also obtained AU$2 million in research funding from the Workers' Compensation Agency.

With regard to the Logan Campus as an example of a partnership with the local educational institutions, businesses and broader community (as well as being funded in a partnership context), the report by Taylor and Blaik (ibid) is interesting. A major conclusion of this report is that 'the Campus is extremely well regarded in the local community, and by its graduates'. Although the report goes on to say that 'local school students…do not look to Griffith University as their preferred tertiary destination' this is perhaps a reflection of the 'newness' of Griffith as compared with the more established universities in the region.

In terms of government-awarded 'linkage grants', those requiring partnerships and financial contributions with industry, the Deputy Vice-Chancellor (Teaching and Learning) Prof. Royce Sadler, indicated that Griffith is 'near the top of the second tier of research universities, after the 'Sandstone' tier'. Approximately 60% of the university's research funding comes from these linkage grants. Major grants also involve

partnerships with such bodies as Family Services (a government agency) and IBM.

There is also at least one major instance of direct funding from industry - a large project funded by AstraZeneca, a Swedish pharmaceutical company providing research funding for biomedical investigations. (www.az.gu.edu.au)

Griffith is fast becoming a nationally significant research-oriented university and attracts high quality research staff from around the world.

Analysis and emerging themes

Our impression is that Griffith has invested the majority of its thought and procedures around the idea of improving education on its local campuses rather than new off-shore markets or partnerships for research (the AstraZeneca partnership is a notable exception). The partnerships with the community around the Logan Campus are less about high funds and high profile and more about becoming part of the local community.

Griffith deliberately admits students who might not be admitted elsewhere and gives them a chance. Probably, because of the extra attention to teaching and learning, these students get opportunities and success rates that would not be possible otherwise. And there are 28,000 of them, so by Dutch and UK standards they are doing well in terms of their student numbers.

There is no longer much attention to purely print-based distance education. Technology is used to improve campus and off campus teaching. Although the focus is on flexible learning, this does not invariably involve high technology; it is more a matter of allowing variations in classroom session conditions, such as more group work (face-to-face). However, all courses have some Web presence.

Scalability and sustainability: The original level of technical support staff at Logan (50) could not be sustained. The strong focus on multimedia development within this team was not scalable to the level of the university as a whole. Web developments have taken resources away from the multimedia approach. Besides targeting larger audiences, sharing resources is another goal of consortia and joint projects that have started.

Management issues around the Logan campus included the fact that the campus was treated as a location and did not have dedicated senior managers who could call in extra resources when needed. Given the ambitious nature of the flexible learning experiment tried at Logan, this was a serious oversight.

The key to achieving the goal of flexible learning is to (1) communicate clearly the message of what is to be done; (2) provide strong leadership responsive to the needs of staff; (3) put greater control of the resources into the hands of the teachers and the learners; and (4) develop a community of academics willing to learn from mistakes and share successes. Merely increasing the ratio of PCs to students will not achieve this.

References

Taylor, P. and Blaik, J., 2002. Logan Campus: What have we learned? 1998 – 2001. Griffith Institute of Higher Education

Recommended web-links

Griffith University
www.gu.edu.au

The ADAPT program
www.gu.edu.au/gfls/adapt/

Logan Campus: What have we learned? 1998-2001, Peter Taylor and Jason Blaik

University/Industry collaboration – AstraZeneca R&D at Griffith University
www.az.gu.edu.au

Peer Review of ICT Teaching Resources
www.peerreview.com.au

10. University of Western Australia: Building on diversity

Arthur Loughran and Bas Cordewener

Context

The University of Western Australia (UWA), which opened in 1913, is located in Perth, the capital city of Western Australia. The university is comprised of 9 faculties serving the academic needs of 14,539 students, of whom 11,128 are full-time and 3,487 are part-time.

The University has a strong research culture and states that 'recently it attracted more competitive research funding on a per capita basis of staff involved in research than any other Australian University.' The emphasis on research is illustrated by the fact that of the (approximately) 1,000 academic staff employed at the university, 30% are employed exclusively in research. The remainder divide their duties between teaching and research. (Annual Report 2000, www.publishing.uwa.edu.au/annualreport/).

The university could be viewed as a traditional university, relying on traditional methods (lectures, tutorials, seminars, laboratory work etc) for teaching and learning activities. In many instances this remains the case. However a surge of activity aimed at reviewing teaching and learning methods was begun in 1997 as a result of an institutional evaluation conducted by a Teaching and Learning Task Force.

University approach to e-Learning

The approach to e-learning at UWA seeks to encourage faculty developments whilst providing a centrally supported system. Also the UWA definition of Managed Learning Environments (MLE) is much broader than that used in the wider academic community. The UWA definition seems to imply that any online system used to support student learning has to be managed,

hence the system is an MLE. A summary of three MLEs in use at UWA is given on the website at (www.catl.uwa.edu.au). These are:

- The Forum (http://forum.uwa.edu.au)
  An in-house environment and offers a variety of modes for the flexible delivery of material. It is primarily used to access digested lectures (audio and video), lecture notes and facilitates online communication via a bulletin board.

- WebCT
  A proprietary VLE administered on behalf of the university by Centre for the Advancement of Teaching and Learning (CATL).

- Jellyfish/Flying Fish
  (http://130.95.52.28/jellyfish).
  A fully diagnostic web-based computer-based tutorial system for maths, engineering and science subjects. The system, which has been progressively developed since 1995, includes error trapping, question severity rating and provides interpretive feedback from the submitted answer. It is used to support approximately 1,000 maths students per annum and it is claimed that it has improved student performance. The system can be purchased for approximately AU$10,000 initial cost, plus AU$1,000 per semester.

Another learning tool that was discussed in detail was a CD-based multimedia resource that provides high school students with a self-paced method for learning classification systems for primates. The School of Anatomy and Human Biology developed the CD supported by a grant from CATL. Evidence was offered to support the claim that there was an improvement in learning due to use of the resources. However comparisons with non-users was not available.

A major element of the UWA portfolio of learning systems is the iLecture initiative. (http://ilectures.uwa.edu.au)

Sixteen lecture theatres are equipped with the facilities to audio record any given lecture. Pictures (captured from a table-top visualiser) and/or PowerPoint slides can also be incorporated into the lecture but not video. The majority, (70%) are audio only.

The lectures are automatically processed into three formats (Real, Windows Media and Quicktime) and stored on a resource database. The processing takes, on average, three hours after which time it can be accessed by all UWA students from a central repository and/or from a course website. Currently lectures are being recorded at the rate of 150 per week. Lectures are normally deleted at the end of the academic year and recorded anew for each session. Evaluation of the impact of iLectures on student outcomes is being conducted.

Lectures are recorded at the discretion of the lecturer. In addition to being used to support student learning they are also to fulfil a staff development function in that they can be used to provide staff with feedback on their lecturing abilities and style. It is claimed that this system can be used to help rationalise provision in those disciplines faced with diminishing student numbers.

Although all UWA students can access the iLecture materials' they are used mainly to supplement the face-to-face tutorial support for students at the Albany regional campus. The campuses were established as out-reach centres aimed at providing regional students with the opportunity to study certain elements of their Natural Resource Management degree programme at local centres. Initially only 4 modules were offered but this has increased to 21 modules for first year students plus a small number for second year students. Some units of the Masters of Education Management postgraduate programme are also now supported by this method.

Support for teaching and learning

The Teaching and Learning Task Force report concluded that the type of structure that UWA needed to support the development of Teaching and Learning included:

- A Centre that was given a clear responsibility to promote and develop FPD in the university.

- Lines of responsibility into the university's organisational structures for teaching and learning.

- A strong bias to working closely in a supportive and enabling role with academic staff at the departmental level.

- Skills in educational technology, learning processes, computer-assisted learning and assessment, course and curriculum design.

A Teaching and Learning Committee has been established. This committee overseas the work of the faculties in this area and, in concert with the faculties, develops university policy in this area.

Since the 1997 report the services aimed at supporting staff to develop new teaching methods has evolved and currently the university's support to staff is channelled through the Organisational and Staff Development Services Unit.

Staff support is provided by three inter-related services. These are:

- Centre for Staff Development (CSD).

- Evaluation of Teaching Unit (TEU).

- Centre for the Advancement of Teaching and Learning (CATL).

CATL is responsible for dealing with issues of flexible learning.

Implementation strategy/structure

When beginning to look at developing online learning, CATL, like many centres of this type, had to take cognisance of a range of issues that militated against the adoption of new methods and technologies for teaching and learning. Some of these issues were:

- Organisational fear,

- Uncertainty about the nature of DL and e-learning,

- Concerns about courses being 'standardised',

- Spectre of job losses,

- Internal competition between different centres.

CATL devised and implemented a plan for the development of online learning that would not only provide a way forward for UWA in this area but would also utilise the existing strengths of UWA and, as a result, significantly reduce concerns about the effects online learning would have on the university and its staff.

Given the devolved faculty structure at UWA a decentralised approach for promoting online learning developments was considered to be suitable. Consequently, a distributed model of support was adopted. The Centre for Advanced Learning and Teaching (CATL) was established in 2000 in order to devise and implement a distributed model of faculty support.

CATL's aim is to encourage and assist with the development and evaluation of faculty-based initiatives and to facilitate the effective university-wide applications of skills and resources developed locally. To achieve this aim CATL has established a University Network for Flexible Teaching and Learning. The Network consists of local appointees (CATLysts) within the faculties who have broad responsibility for promoting teaching and learning within the faculty and work with others within the Network to promote teaching and learning within the broader UWA community.

Teaching and learning approaches

CATL acts as a central hub that provides administrative, planning and coordination support to the faculty based individuals who are known as 'CATLysts'. Each CATLyst is an academic member of their respective faculty with duties divided between work for the faculty (50%), eg teaching commitment, and CATL (50%).

They act as in-faculty staff developers whose primary tasks are:

- to provide advice to their faculty, via the faculty teaching and learning committee, on issues relating to developing flexible learning to suit faculty needs (not necessarily the same as university needs);

- to facilitate development of online learning 'products', e.g. use of multimedia and VLEs, with individual faculty staff;

- to facilitate relationships between academic staff and learning asset production units;

- to provide feedback for the development of the central CATL service.

As part of the promotion activities, CATL provides funds to support faculty teaching and learning research and/or development projects. CATL has a fund of AU$150,000 per annum, which is allocated, in sums of AU$10,000, AU$25,000 and AU$50,000.

The faculty must approve project applications from individual staff before they can be put forward for a CATL grant. This ensures that the needs of the faculty are taken into consideration. It has been noted that the project themes are moving from ICT issues to more fundamental teaching and learning issues.

CATL has completed 2 years of a 3 year programme and in that time has helped the university move incrementally from a concept of flexible programme delivery to one of flexible teaching and learning thereby raising critical awareness about teaching and learning methods in general and at the same time reducing fears about the negative effects of change. An example of the change in culture is that in some cases faculty will provide direct project funding if the project applications for CATL funding are not successful or if successful application are not awarded a high enough grant.

Although CATL is not responsible for the development of e-learning within UWA they do provide a co-ordinating role for such developments and for disseminating information about online/e-learning. They fulfil their dissemination role by providing information via the CATL website (www.catl.uwa.edu.au). This website contains a range of information about teaching and learning activities and related information.

Analysis and emerging themes

It can be concluded that UWA is a thriving, faculty centric university. Promotion of teaching and learning is the responsibility of a central service but significant developments, e.g. iLectures, are due largely to the enthusiasm of faculty based individuals supported by the resources faculty based asset production units of which there are six listed (www.catl.uwa.edu.au/flexible/support.html).

Attempts have been made to provide tailored assistance to faculty staff by establishing the CATLyst model. Evidence of the success of this model is not readily available. However there is strong evidence of growing interest into research in teaching and learning during academic year 2001/2002. During that time period CALT awarded two major grants of AU$50,000 and AU$40,000 respectively plus a further 10 grants of approximately AU$10,000 each.

Overall it is reasonable to assume that there will be no significant change in the structure of teaching and learning development at UWA in the foreseeable future.

Recommended web-links

Annual Report 2000
www.publishing.uwa.edu.au/annualreport/

University of Western Australia
www.uwa.edu.au

Centre for Advanced Learning and Teaching (CATL) **www.catl.uwa.edu.au**

The Forum
http://forum.uwa.edu.au)

Jellyfish/Flying Fish
http://130.95.52.28/jellyfish

iLectures
http://ilectures.uwa.edu.au

11. WestOne Services: Utilising technology for learning and managing associated change

Robert Harding

Context

WestOne is not a college or indeed any sort of HE institution. It is best seen as an agency, set up by the State of Western Australia, whose role is to 'support the Western Australian vocational sector in utilising technology for learning and managing associated change'. WestOne works with TAFE (Technical and Further Education) Colleges and sees itself as 'a conduit for service provision across the WA (Western Australian) VET (Vocational Education and Training) sector'. WestOne was set up in August 1999.

Background to VET in Australia

Funding

Funding in the VET Sector in Australia comes 33% from the Federal Government (Commonwealth), 67% from the State in question. This can lead to some interesting politics since the political complexion of States often differs from that of the Federal Government. (At the time of our visit, all the States are Labour governed whilst the Federal Government is Conservative.)

Framework

Stuart Young, (Director products & technology) thinks that the Australian VET sector is probably the most highly organised vocational sector in the world. Though States make their own decisions, there is the ANTA (Australian National Training Agency), which is the channel for Federal funds. In fact the VET sector was under siege from a reform agenda for decade. This has led to the setting up of a number of training packages: these define various competencies and how to measure them.

Despite the theoretical possibility of considerable variation across States (because of their political independence), there are strong inter-state links and many areas of collaboration (e.g. e-Learning and content). There is a useful ATQF (Australian Training Quality Framework) that is universally accepted.

WestOne's mission and development

Drivers for WestOne's strategy

The State and National consensus is that the VET system must assist Australia to make the transition to the 'information environment'. This requires that the sector delivers:

- Skills to thrive (e.g. in existing industries).

- Skills to work in new information industries.

- Skills for emerging industries, with changing work practices and preferences.

There is a National 'Flexible Learning Advisory Group' (FLAG), of which Stuart Young is a member. FLAG has produced the AFL (Australian Flexible Learning) Framework, with a blueprint for flexible training for Information Technology and Economics. This has a 5-year plan for the years 2000-4, with annual strategies[1], and the ultimate aim is to position Australia as a world leader in exploiting the opportunities afforded by the 'information environment'. This is expressed by the 'formula':

Intelligent competition + collaboration = competitive advantage

which is to achieve:

- shared benefits;

- strategic use of new technologies;

81

---

1 See http://flexiblelearning.net.au/projectevolve.htm

- accelerated pick-up of new technologies;

- strategic partnerships;

- leveraged investment;

- and be demand driven.

WestOne's strategy and goals

A key principle in WestOne's tactics for getting itself up and running was to cost all desired targets and goals. This was to ensure that WestOne's parent agency and its advisers considered all targets and goals carefully. WestOne did not want to be charged with delivering anything that 'looked like a good idea' without a proper consideration of costs and benefits.

WestOne particularly stresses its mission to help TAFE colleges meet five areas of importance from the AFL list:

- Professional Development, especially in connection with Learnscope[2].

- Supportive Technology Infrastructure.

- Online content and units.

- Enabling policies (e.g. digital copyright).

- Legal and Regulatory Framework.

Getting up and running

WestOne's products and services were to be free to State-funded colleges, but it was not to be mandatory for Colleges to use these. WestOne did not attempt to satisfy all possible shades of demand but rather looked at the needs of one or two colleges in detail and then came up with a coherent overall plan for its services.

This has been a very successful strategy in that every TAFE college in Western Australia now uses WestOne's services.

What WestOne offers

Pressures on TAFE colleges

The pressures on TAFE colleges reported to us by WestOne are:

- Cultural & economic developments;

- Federal and State Policy;

- Globalisation;

- Changing world of work;

- Demand for new Flexible Training products;

- New business opportunities.

A TAFE college's primary customers are students, industry and business. These customers want a service that is:

- Convenient.

- Timely.

- Self-paced etc.

WestOne set itself the task of helping TAFE colleges to meet these demands. An eLearning solution was seen as the most effective course of action. Colleges had considerable difficulties in adopting eLearning solutions because generally they lacked sufficient internal technical expertise and support, and also because their teaching staff were unfamiliar and untrained in the use of e-Learning. Therefore WestOne saw that it needed to offer strong support for some key activities:

- Help colleges to put web front ends on the Managed Learning Environment (MLE) backends run by other people.

- Rapid development methodologies.

2 See http://flexiblelearning.net.au/vlc/cocoon/ls/display_Stories/1-90000/1201-1500/display_Stories_1371_0.html.
  In particular, 'Each year, funding is provided by the Australian National Training Authority (ANTA) to teams within registered training organisations in the vocational education and training sector to undertake work-based programs focussed on their professional development in the area of flexible delivery and online delivery.'

- Design help for websites (prior to WestOne, college websites were often little more than 'brochure ware').

- Setting up customer self-service portals.

General description of WestOne's support

This is well described by Stuart Young's own picture of WestOne, quoted verbatim below:

"As an institution specially created to support the Western Australian vocational sector in utilising technology for learning and managing associated change, WestOne has a major role in working with TAFE (Technical and Further Education) Colleges and other organisations to address the challenges of the Knowledge Economy.

"Established in August 1999, WestOne Services (WestOne) is an Institution under the terms of the Vocational Education and Training Act and under the management and control of the Director General of the Department of Training.

"In the State vocational education and training sector, WestOne is the leader in the application of new technologies to the teaching and learning experience. WestOne is the only dedicated training institute in Western Australia with experience and capability in the rapidly converging audio-visual, print and online media technologies.

"WestOne has a major role working with TAFE Colleges and other organizations in addressing the challenges of the emerging Knowledge Economy. In formalising, enhancing and packaging the delivery of learning materials over the Internet, WestOne is a conduit for service provision across the WA (Western Australian) VET sector. Audio-visual facilities at WestOne produce and broadcast a wide range of TAFE award courses and Adult and Community Education (ACE) programs, and provide a platform for satellite-based transmissions via Channel 31. Print facilities at WestOne publish, source and distribute state and national learning and training materials.

"In response to its operational environment, WestOne has forged a collaborative organisational style and an identity as a leader in customer-focused service and the use of innovative educational technology. WestOne relies on strong client partnerships and the use of collaboration to manage constructive change.

"WestOne strives to provide cost-effective individual learning solutions to meet vocational education and training needs by working with partners to source, develop, produce and distribute state-of-the-art learning resources and technology enabled learning solutions. A wide range of flexible learning options and career opportunities are facilitated, and collaborators are assisted and supported in applying the power of digital technology to provide efficient, customer-focused training programs, processes and services.

"Significant effort is being put into creating new training markets through extended and improved access to high quality products, services and strategic capability. WestOne will continue to closely work with VET providers to facilitate the mainstreaming of technology enabled learning strategies and leverage the increased uptake of flexible training options as online Internet (data) and entertainment (broadcast) capabilities converge into an unprecedented range of learning delivery media and mode options for individuals and enterprises."

Analysis and emerging themes

- The visiting group was interested in some specific aspects of WestOne's services. For example, WestOne chose WebCT for its Managed Learning Environment service on the grounds that this was the most widely used MLE in Australia (i.e. their policy was to go for the widest degree of compatibility).

- WestOne does not currently offer an online assessment service for colleges to use.

- We also asked what in WestOne's opinion was needed to make online provision fully effective, to which their answer was that it is a good support function that is required, and WestOne provides this to colleges.

- We asked about the size of WestOne. It has 50 employees altogether, but very few in IT (only two in fact) and only 6-8 in products and services. These two functions are largely met by contracting out the work.

Issues raised by WestOne

VET qualifications are not intended to compete with, or be seen as, equivalent to degrees. There was some talk of this (we are not sure when – perhaps whilst the AFL Framework was being debated), but it was certainly opposed by universities and eventually VET qualifications were given quite a distinct and separate identity.

WestOne observes that a significant portion of students enroll for complete courses but in fact only complete certain units, and do not stay on the course. They interpret this as indicating that students are looking to improve certain specific skills, rather than wanting to obtain qualifications.

WestOne sees employer influence on syllabus content as not always beneficial to wider education. This is because of the way assessment is done in the VET sector: it is necessarily workplace-based (as indeed is the case in the UK). On-the-job and off-the-job assignments are blended, but the feeling is that many of the training packages are driven by the bigger commercial organisations (because they can afford to send representatives to the working parties), even though, in aggregate, they may not be the major employers. Though this involvement brings some benefits, there are some drawbacks. One example quoted was the shortage of some fundamental and basic computer science materials, the emphasis being instead on training for specific applications.

Although WestOne has successfully established itself as the eLearning service provider for all TAFE colleges in Western Australia, they would like to see more 'mainstreaming' of the materials they have developed. They estimate that they have about 7,000 hours of these.

Visiting Team's overall impressions

Relationships

We have already mentioned that Australian Universities adopted a 'keep out' policy towards VET qualifications. That and the apparently 'most highly organised vocational sector in the world' suggests a distinct separation between the VET sector and universities. On the other hand, what WestOne told us suggests that the VET sector is highly responsive to the needs of businesses and of individuals who require professional development, and that they keep in tune with society's needs in this respect both through VET sector bodies (such as FLAG) and through direct contacts with business.

Were the objectives clear?

The visiting team found WestOne's objectives impressively clear, and based on a penetrating analysis of business and political circumstances.

How well were they achieved?

Our short visit did not permit us time to hear directly from WestOne's customers, the TAFE colleges, but our impression was highly favourable.

What do we want to 'borrow'?

The approach 'we'll supply what you need, not necessarily what you now think you need' is a bold one and carries certain risks but, as WestOne has shown, if this approach is used with open eyes it can be very successful.

Collaboration opportunities?

WestOne appears to be very well set up to produce quality distance learning materials at excellent value-for-money prices, certainly lower than UK prices.

Recommended web-links

WestOne's home website and online, television, etc course information
www.westone.wa.gov.au/

WestOne's careers website
www.getaccess.wa.gov.au/

Online enrolments for courses developed by WestOne
www.challengertafe.wa.edu.au/

Vocational handbook online developed by WestOne
http://tafehandbook.westone.wa.gov.au/

Online access to student results, website and student authentication developed by WestOne
http://central.tafe.wa.edu.au/

Course catalogue/searching developed by WestOne for all colleges
http://central.tafe.wa.edu.au/frameset-main-course.html

Site for cross-sectional education and training
www.edna.edu.au/

FLAG's 5-year plan annual strategies
http://flexiblelearning.net.au/projectevolve.htm

About Learnscope
http://flexiblelearning.net.au/vlc/cocoon/ls/display_Stories/1-90000/1201 1500/display_Stories_1371_0.html

12. University of Melbourne: ICT to transform the curriculum

Janet Hanson and Martin Valcke

Context

The University of Melbourne was established in 1853, the second Australian university to be established. It is a large, multi-campus university with over 37,000 students. There are approximately 2,000 academic staff and 2,400 general staff. The university is divided into eleven faculties covering most disciplines, and includes the School of Graduate Studies and the Melbourne Business School. It is a leading research university, being the first in Australia to award PhDs in 1948. The main aim of the 'Melbourne Agenda' is to develop the University of Melbourne as a 'broad-based research and teaching university of world renown'. This vision, as expressed by Vice-Chancellor, Alan Gilbert, is "of a University of Melbourne international in character and focus, attracting the highest quality staff and students from around Australia and internationally, producing research and scholarship to a standard matching that of the best universities in the world". Some 18% of its students are from overseas, mainly from South East Asia. Its success in strongly positioning itself internationally has been recognised through the award of the 2001-2002 Good Universities Guides 'Australian University of the Year', the focus of which is International Standing.

e-Learning and the mission of the university

The University has been encouraging the use of learning technologies in its teaching programmes for a relatively long time now. This is seen largely as way of improving the quality and flexibility of face-to-face teaching and only secondarily as an efficiency measure. There appears to be little interest in developing distance education, outside a few specific areas such as Agriculture and Education. The focus of development to date has been, notably, on multimedia. This, although broadly defined, tends to be interpreted as computer-aided learning resources for use by students studying at the University's campuses. One of the targets from the 2002 Operational Plan was to have 70% of academic staff in each department using multimedia in their teaching. Another was that the proportion of students responding positively to use of multimedia should be not less than 70%. In pursuit of these targets, a broader consideration of the use of the Web and Virtual Learning Environments (VLE) in teaching has started to emerge more recently.

At present, a combination of commercial and in-house learning environments is in use. The principal in-house platform is WebRAFT (Web Resources Automated for Teaching). This purports to provide a secure and reliable web-based delivery system to support online teaching and learning which is fully integrated with Merlin and staff/student email systems. It provides an easy-to-use, 'zero-administration' web-site to enable academics to focus on content issues. Student enrolments are automatic and subject co-ordinators can upload their materials from their desktop using CAP or FTP. Features such as student/group publishing, CD-ROM image creation and online conferencing form a basic core of services which academics and their support staff can use as an online collaborative teaching environment. Another in-house system is OCCA (Online Course Component Architecture) which is a general purpose database/server system for creating customised learning and teaching environments.

At the time of our visit in March 2002, we were informed that the university was intending to introduce the new version of WebCT, VISTA, as a university-wide learning platform, which is the current learning environment in use at Monash. However, a more recent report on the university's web-site suggests that this is being reconsidered.

'At the 2002 Lindenderry Planning and Budget Conference, held in June, it was decided to postpone the funding to implement WebCT Vista. Planning and Budget Committee requested that the Information Division use this opportunity to investigate and evaluate a range of systems for courseware delivery and the creation of effective teaching and learning environments. The Teaching, Learning and Research Support Department of the Information Division will undertake intensive evaluation of a range of options.' www.infodiv.unimelb.edu.au/telars/lms/index.html

Two specific strategic partnerships also appear to be influencing the direction of the development of e-learning at Melbourne. These are the partnership with Monash University and Melbourne's membership of Universitas 21(U21).

Implementation strategy

Melbourne adopted a long-term strategy from 1997 to transform teaching and learning through the use of multimedia and educational technology. Broad ranging funding for innovators through the 'Teaching and Learning – Multimedia and Educational Technology' programme (T&L (M&ET)) was offered initially. This was followed by more targeted funding to cover specific priorities, for example, collaborative projects relating to the Melbourne-Monash protocol. So far, about AU$10 million has been awarded to around 218 development projects. Achievement of the ambitious strategic targets relating to the use of learning technologies in the curriculum become realistic when one considers the scale of this investment. The allocation of funds is based on a competitive bidding system. Initially individual academics submitted project proposals but more recently there is a need to demonstrate how projects are linked to faculty priorities. About 50% of the projects are now thought to focus more on the use of generic tools that might have a wider impact beyond the originating faculty. The T&L (M&ET) Committee oversees the programme. (http://talmet.unimelb.edu.au/).

A mixed mode of technical and pedagogic support from within the faculties and from the re-organised central services is being provided. This has been accompanied by a thorough and long-term evaluation strategy with three reports produced to date (Taylor, 1998; James, 2000; Fritze, 2002).

In keeping with the research orientation of the university and the desire to disseminate good practice, there is a strong focus on publishing evaluation reports about the individual projects. We were told of a target to work towards three research publications related to each project. Fritze's 2002 report is a meta-analysis of 84 of these publications.

Despite the added incentive of support for IPR for academics who are developing e-learning resources, the uptake differs widely among the faculties. At the time of our visit, the School of Medicine was regarded as the one where multimedia was used most frequently. A report from the University Council in June 2002 on performance against 2001 targets suggested that:

'The University has had variable success in achieving its aims for incorporating Internet and multimedia teaching methods as an integral part of its program. General information indicates that at least 50% of academic staff make use of multimedia in their teaching.'

Support for teaching and learning

Central services supporting teaching and learning

In common with many other universities we visited, Melbourne had recently experienced changes to the organisation of its central support for teaching and learning. The Information Division was created in 2000 with responsibility for the development and management of information systems, library and teaching materials, and multimedia resources and for the development and operation of the communications infrastructure. It is an excellent example of how the synergy between IT Services, Library and Educational Development can be encouraged and enhanced.

Within the Division, support for learning and teaching is integrated under the umbrella of the Department of Teaching, Learning and Research Support (TeLaRS), (www.infodiv.unimelb.edu.au/telars). This umbrella structure reflects the clear research orientation of this university, but also shows how quality is actively pursued in the field of teaching and learning. Five sub-sections of TeLaRS provide specific support as follows:

Courseware development

This unit offers professional support for the design of multimedia products. Its 17 academic and technical staff offers services to projects under the T&L(M&ET) programme and they also work on large commercial productions. The

products were, until recently, mainly CD-ROMs but it now supports the development of web-based learning environments. They were responsible for the development of OCCA (Online Course Component Architecture).

Flexible learning delivery services

This small unit of 3 staff supports academics who are seeking to adopt flexible approaches to learning, to enhance their teaching through technology and to engage their students in collaborative learning. It provides a range of services, programs and development resources for staff and students through the innovative Percy Baxter Collaborative Learning Centre which is situated within the Library.

Innovation case study

The Percy Baxter Collaborative Learning Centre

(www.infodiv.unimelb.edu.au/telars/flds/pbclc.html)

The Percy Baxter Collaborative Learning Centre has been established by the Information Division as a learning resource that provides a range of services, programmes and development resources both to students and academic staff. It provides support for staff wanting to enhance their teaching through technology, it provides resources for students to enable them to develop information skills and it provides well-equipped, flexible spaces where staff and students can engage in collaborative learning activities together.

The Centre hosts a number of programmes that focus on the development of skills in information literacy and technology-enhanced teaching and learning. Information literacy skills are developed through enabling students and staff to access electronic journals and web-based resources. A range of tools for staff and students to develop multimedia and web-based resources is also provided.

Academic staff are offered a range of professional development programmes including communication and collaboration on the Web, working with sound, pictures and movies and using web cameras.

Resources are also available for students to work collaboratively in small groups, both face-to-face and in collaborative online environments. A wireless network enables access to the Internet using laptop computers.

The Centre is located within the Library and provides an excellent example of the way in which Melbourne is encouraging a collaborative learning culture among staff and students.

Learning resources services

The main function of this group of 17 librarians and multimedia specialists is to support staff who want to integrate electronic resource discovery into their programmes. This reflects a clear shift away from the view of a traditional library to a learning environment where students and staff engage in a collaborative way on tasks. There is an aim to integrate information literacy skills into the subject teaching which builds on the Australian Information Literacy Standards. The service is attempting to gain endorsement by the university for incorporating these into the list of generic skills required of its graduate students. It is involved in a Council of Australian University Librarians (CAUL) project to develop a tool to measure outcomes of Information Literacy programs in Universities (www.infodiv.unimelb.edu.au/telars/lru/init0102.html#Rationale).

Research and evaluation services

This group of 5 staff supports academics in evaluating the effectiveness of technology integration into their teaching. A typical example of an evaluation study is the Report on the Evaluation of ICT Initiative in Education (Fritze, 2002). This is a grounded theory evaluation study of the papers published about the projects in the T&L(M&ET) programme. The report and the database of findings are available online at http://talmet.unimelb.edu.au/.

Intellectual property issues

The University of Melbourne presents an impressive example of how intellectual property rights and copyright may be approached. From a situation where there was hardly any co-ordination, there is now a centralised, co-ordinated approach. Models are available to cope with commercialisation and licensing and the multimedia products are a prime target for this service.

Centre for the study of higher education (CSHE)

CSHE is a national and international leader in higher education policy research and educational development. For more than 30 years CSHE has provided independent, research-based advice and support on matters of teaching and learning, the student experience, professional development for academics, and quality assurance policies and processes. The Centre undertakes research projects for the State and Federal governments as well as for the university. It provides a range of professional development workshops and seminars for university staff and is responsible for the university's Program for Excellence in Teaching and Learning (PETL). (www.cshe.unimelb.edu.au/)

Teaching and learning approaches

During our visit we were not aware of one single generic approach to learning and teaching which could be said to be driving the e-learning activities. It was apparent that the autonomy of the individual member of academic staff was paramount but there were indications of an emerging consensus. For example, many of the multimedia projects in the School of Medicine adopt a problem-based learning approach. Fritze also has reported evidence of 'significant moves to transform curricular through pbl and also student directed learning and the use of authentic contexts, group and collaborative work.' (Fritze, 2002, Executive summary). The resources devoted to the Percy Baxter Centre would seem to support this move. As already suggested, there was little evidence of a move towards distance education, except, for example in the School of Agriculture, where provision over several campuses provided the impetus. In recognition of this diversity, but also in an attempt to provide a shared view, the clearest statement of an approach to learning and teaching for Melbourne has emerged since our visit through a publication entitled 'Nine Principles Guiding Teaching and Learning in the University of Melbourne' (James and Baldwin, 2002). This aims to provide a statement on the scholarship of teaching and learning in a research-led university and a reference guide to good practice and university resources.

Partnerships

Partnerships are important to Melbourne and operate on a more extensive scale than we observed in many other universities visited.

Locally, a collaborative protocol has been drawn up between Melbourne and Monash University. www.unimelb.edu.au/about/melbmonash/. One of the aims is to exploit new teaching and learning technologies in curriculum and courseware development to provide more flexible approaches to learning for students.

Melbourne is responding to the pressures of internationalisation through its membership of the Universitas 21 network, which 'provides a framework for international collaboration, capitalising on the established reputation and operational reach of each of its members.' www.universitas.edu.au/introduction.html.

One of the activities involves contributing to the U21 Learning Resource Catalogue (LRC) http://lrc.infodiv.unimelb.edu.au, an initiative that aims to facilitate the sharing and reuse of learning objects. Through the creation of separate but interoperable databases of information (metadata) describing learning resources developed at each institution, the LRC seeks to enable an efficient use of existing resources, encourage collaboration between U21 partners, and to reduce replication in the creation of costly learning materials.

By deliberate choice, the university has rejected the strategy of establishing international branch campuses. It is also de-emphasising strategies for delivering awards internationally online, although it may do this in selected disciplines or indirectly through Melbourne University Private, www.muprivate.edu.au/index.asp. This is a private university subsidiary of the University of Melbourne. Its core activities are targeted at corporate clients. Its development has not been without controversy, see, for example, www.muprivate.edu.au/PDF/ MUPrivateFacts.pdf

Analysis and emerging issues

The University of Melbourne clearly presents itself as a top research institution. Nevertheless it seems to be able to combine this with growing attention paid to high-quality teaching and learning. This justifies the large amounts of seed money made available to start up ICT-related development projects.

The high levels of ICT-usage are being encouraged strategically through organisational and structural changes in the way the university functions. The integration of service departments is a typical example of this, which seems to make the innovation scaleable and sustainable. Nevertheless, questions are being asked about the budget provisions to further support the projects. Sustainability is not yet reached in this context.

The university stresses strategic partnerships. It will be interesting to see what impact this has on its future e-learning developments.

An emerging emphasis on problem-based and collaborative learning approaches is matched by a similar emphasis on enabling students to take advantage of these new learning strategies.

The university leads the way on IPR and copyright issues, which are likely to become more important within the context of web-based learning but also in the context of the partnerships.

References

Fritze, P. 2002. Report on the evaluation of ICT initiatives in Education.
http://talmet.unimelb.edu.au/pages/ICTeval_exec_sum.htm

James, R. and Baldwin, G., 2002. Nine principles guiding teaching and learning at the University of Melbourne.
www.unimelb.edu.au/ExecServ/whac/appg0302.pdf

James, R., 2000. Status report on the impact on teaching and learning of Multimedia and Educational Technology development grants. CSHE. (only available within the University)

Taylor, J., 1998. Strategies for transforming teaching and learning using multimedia: cultural change in university teaching. The University of Melbourne.

Recommended web-links

Home Page of University of Melbourne web-site
www.unimelb.edu.au/

University of Melbourne Strategic Plan: Perspective 2001.
www.unimelb.edu.au/vc/stratplan/

Operational Plan 2002
www.unimelb.edu.au/vc/opplan/

Alan Gilbert, Vice-Chancellor. A vision for Melbourne.
www.unimelb.edu.au/vc/

The Melbourne and Monash Protocol - A Proposal for Collaborative Endeavours
www.unimelb.edu.au/about/melbmonash/

Grants for collaborative learning and teaching projects
http://talmet.unimelb.edu.au/melbmonash/

The Department of Teaching, Learning and Research Support (TeLaRS)
www.infodiv.unimelb.edu.au/telars/

13. Monash University: On the road to a prestigious, private university

Bas Cordewener and Jan van der Veen

Context

Named after prominent Australian, Sir John Monash, Monash University was established by an Act of Parliament in 1958 making it the first university to be established in the state of Victoria for 106 years. Since its first intake of students in 1961, Monash has grown from a single campus at Clayton to six campuses in Australia, one in Malaysia and one in South Africa.

The university is one of the largest Australian universities and is a member of the Group of Eight (large and prestigious 'leading' Australian Universities). Government money covers 35% of the university income. Other funds are mostly generated by full fee-paying students in Australia and abroad. Monash has a number of campuses in the Melbourne area, but also in Malaysia and Southern Africa. Furthermore centres are opening in the UK, Italy and Germany. About 50,000 students are enrolled in a wide variety of programmes. This number includes 11,000 off campus students. Approximately 6,000 people are employed by Monash.

e-Learning and the mission of the university

The policy of the university is to be a high quality university, independent from government policies. To reach the goals of the university Monash is expanding its world-wide market. Diversification is strived for as a means to be less vulnerable if parts of the market are not favourable in a certain period. The need to invest in IT projects is recognised. The investments in this area are estimated at AU$16 million.

Support for teaching and learning

Support for staff and departments is organised via the Centre for Learning & Teaching Support (CeLTS), which provides a Graduate Certificate in Higher Education (particularly for new staff), and among other topics also WebCT training. CeLTS mission is ' to further the achievement of University and Faculty objectives with respect to student-centred flexible learning and teaching in accordance with the Monash Plan and the Learning and Teaching Plan'. CeLTS activities include: quality improvement of teaching and learning via staff development and consultation; research into new technologies and distance learning; the production of multimedia materials within a pedagogical framework (multimedia unit); evaluation services; curriculum design; assessment; and student support such as language support for students with a non-English speaking background and learning skills training. The multimedia unit develops graphics and animations (Flash) which enrich course components in need of visualisations and animations. There is no significant database or procedure to easily find re-usable components yet, but awareness is growing. The units of CeLTS are located at different sites due to the fact that Monash has several campuses.

As WebCT has recently been introduced university-wide, many staff need to be trained. This was organised via CeLTS who also plan to provide follow up workshops so that staff can better utilise the facilities that WebCT can offer. WebCT and other IT support is offered to students and staff via the university portal, called my.monash. Besides WebCT, a home-made system called Interlearn is available for those faculties preferring this system. Online video and in particular audio of lectures is supported by a streaming media server. Discussion groups are facilitated by a Collabra server.

The central overhead for administration, infrastructure and support services is 32%. Overhead at the faculty level adds another 8-18% depending on the nature of the faculty. The policy is to move to activity-based costing so as to have a better overview of real costs and benefits. It is not the intention that all activities are self-supporting.

Teaching and learning approaches

The two main themes in teaching and learning that are promoted within Monash are flexibility and student-centred learning. Flexibility is used to enable Monash to target different groups with different needs. For example, undergraduates and lawyers in continuing education are both served, but using completely different formats. Monash offers different combinations of on campus, hybrid and fully online programs and subjects. Distance students are served by a combination of paper-based materials, CD-ROMs and online support. A tendency can be seen for fully online modules to opt for some face-to-face options as well in particular for skills, thus moving to more hybrid instructional designs. The Faculty of Business and Economics has pooled all of its course arrangements and resources so that these can then be reused or tailored by all staff for new groups of learners. In the main course programmes, special attention is paid to the need to teach generic student skills. Special short courses on a wide variety of topics are open for students. Student-centred learning is implemented in different ways. Medicine is implementing problem-based learning.

If Monash is to achieve its expansion plans it must target different cultural groups, and so much attention is given to the cultural aspects of delivering education. For example, to "make sure that female Muslim students are taught by female staff".

Implementation strategy

IT Support (ITS) is in charge of the tele-learning infrastructure. This includes servers running WebCT (now 120 courses active) and Interlearn, but also a number of video-conferencing units. Teacher support is organised via CeLTS. The co-ordination of the support and infrastructure organised via CeLTS and ITS is in the hands of the Flexible Learning and Teaching (FLT) unit. The FLT unit defines projects with project leaders and teams with members from relevant units. It reports to the Vice-Chancellor of Academic Affairs. Monash seems to recognise that there is an expertise in Learning and Teaching Support that is distinct from both the academic disciplines to which it is applied and from the technology used to deliver it. The FLT unit separates strategic institutional level policy making (undertaken or mediated by the FLT unit) from the more specific expertise-related decisions that must be made by the faculties, CeLTS and IT Services.

Strategic decisions in relation to IT & education are defined in the Electronically Supported Teaching and Learning (ESTL) committee with higher management from central and faculty level present. This strategic steering committee also monitors new technologies and tries to raise awareness within Monash regarding IT issues.

Support details for the faculties are defined by support level agreements that originate from neatly described project methodologies and service methodologies.

At the faculty level the Dean and the Faculty Board are responsible for the educational activities and the innovations planned for. Some faculties organise seminars for their staff on teaching, IT and management topics. After a first year of implementation of WebCT it is anticipated that staff will be used to these new technologies, and faculties intend to make a next step introducing quality improvements into their online education. It is expected that the next step will bring about more specialism within the teaching profession, which hopefully will mean the start of a cultural change: not only academic staff will have control over the subject. The question still is whether scaling up from the pilot situation to a broader use of WebCT will take off sufficiently in the less IT-focussed faculties where power is devolved and faculty operate rather anonymously.

After the provision of sufficient support, an important priority is the recognition of teaching achievements in terms of promotion so as to have a balance between the recognition for research, entrepreneurship and teaching. In the more traditional settings also a cultural change is needed to shift focus to flexible and (partly) online education.

In some content areas (Law for example) consortia like Open Learning Australia are formed with Griffith University and others so as to enable students to pick and choose a set of modules. Some students take as many modules as is required for either a Griffith or Monash degree, so-called co-branding strategies.

The information provided to staff and students is organised via a portal (my.monash, see Figure 6: http://monash.edu/portal/integration.html). The intention is to direct the support at requested services and not so much in terms of underlying applications. The model in Figure 6 describes the 'aimed at' situation with a single user logon. This has been partially achieved.

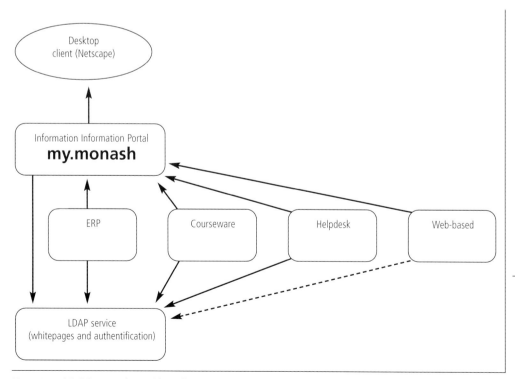

Figure 6. Model of the Monash Portal for staff and students.

Quality at Monash

Quality management and evaluation research have been prioritised by Monash management, both as a means for quality improvement as well as for accreditation purposes. The unit for quality management is called Centre for Higher Education Quality (CHEQ). It is recognised that claims for high or even best quality need to be backed up by data and other evidence. The seven core values and principles of quality management at Monash are:

- creating the agenda (fitness for purpose);

- quality as a professional responsibility;

- encouraging the development of a learning organisation;

- valuing diversity, devolution and comparable treatment;

- an open and informed approach to quality;

- a planned and systematic approach to quality;

- valuing self-reflection and external reference.

Among other items, the CHEQ evaluation research portfolio includes: subject evaluation, research into student experiences, employer satisfaction surveys and expert evaluations of graduates and postgraduate programs.

Quality improvement is proudly seen as a (commercial) selling point. On the other hand it is clear that all initiatives to innovate and increase the quality of education are balanced against the expected raise in revenues for the university.

The library

As part of the introduction to the library and information retrieval skills not online, live introductions are organised. Glossaries and 'how to' information can be found via the online virtual library tours (www.lib.monash.edu.au/).

Besides the books and (e-)journals, the library offers collaborative learning workplaces for students. Search portals, research profiles, WebCT suggestions, digitalisation of reading materials and the composition of reading lists are facilities offered to the staff by the library. A special feature is the automated recording of lectures in 20 lecture theatres, which are online 3 minutes after closing time of the lectures.

Analysis and emerging issues

From the visit to Monash a number of issues emerged. These issues are merged with comments and observations of the UK / Netherlands-visitors.

- Monash has seen a decrease of government funding. It has successfully found new markets in an entrepreneurial way resulting in a situation with only 35% of income coming from the government. Apparently not all Faculties have the same prospects. By nature Business, Economics, Law and Medicine (80% are full-fee students!) can penetrate the market better than, for example, Science and Arts. However, the latter can also find niches on the market such as 'communications and media studies'. Although this commercial setting involves some employer pressure on content and process, clearly at Monash the commitment to academic skills and feasible instructional designs is alive.

- Like many other institutions, Monash has identified the need to co-ordinate IT support and Teaching & Learning support. However Monash has implemented this co-ordination at both the strategic level (ESTL), as well as the implementation level (FLT). There is a strong belief that once the use of Information Communication Technology (ICT) and applications like WebCT has begun in a modest way, fuelled by organisational and economical advantages, this process will lead to greater cultural and pedagogical changes.

- Likewise, quality management is set on the agenda via a separate body, which prepares the quality audits by developing tools and methods, and aim at supporting faculties in their preparation for audits planned for 2004. The intention to support strategy and management in a more data-driven way is clearly inevitable in an environment that claims to deliver high quality education.

- The Web-presence of Monash offers a tremendous wealth of information for the different target groups. This is not only very helpful for visitors. It also supports the shared and growing body of knowledge of the university itself.

Recommended web-links

Monash University, Melbourne Australia
http://monash.edu/

Centre for Learning & Teaching Support (CeLTS)
www.celts.monash.edu.au/

Portal (my.monash, see figure 6)
http://monash.edu/portal/integration.html

Library
www.lib.monash.edu.au/

14. Deakin University: Institutional consolidation

Martin Jenkins and Wiebe Nijlunsing

Context

Deakin University has a network of six campuses across Melbourne and the regional Victorian cities of Geelong and Warrnambool; and was established in Geelong in 1974.

Following a series of institutional mergers the university has grown in size and scope. It now employs 1,955 staff and has more than 30,000 students enrolled in a wide range of courses across its campuses. There are a further 43,000 students enrolled through Deakin Australia, mainly involved in professional development programs which are offered on a fee-paying basis in partnership with various professional associations, government and industry.

Deakin University has five faculties: Arts; Business and Law; Education; Science and Technology; and Health and Behavioural Sciences. Each faculty has a series of schools based on discipline areas. Deakin University has research programs associated with each discipline area. Areas of research concentration include: chiral chemistry; molecular and heavy metal biology; adaptive computing systems; metal manufacturing; physical activity and metabolism in health and disease; citizenship and international relations; flexible learning and educational program delivery; sustainable regional development; and socio-cultural change.

Deakin University is 25 years old and was set up for distance education in Victoria with a mandate from the start for having on and off campus students and providing equity between them. The model adopted for distance education was borrowed from the Open University with the use of course teams to develop materials, there has always been a focus on technology even with the initial audio visual (AV) and print materials. Many courses were developed for distance education first and then transferred to on campus delivery. This has led to a culture which makes it easier to adopt new technologies for teaching and learning.

e-Learning and the mission of the university

The university is committed to offering flexible study opportunities and courses are available on and off campus and through full and part-time study or a combination of modes. Initial Deakin developments with distance learning were print based, the university was set up with the mission to provide equity between campus-based and off campus students. Deakin put in place (a long time ago) a policy that teachers had to teach in both distance learning and face-to-face format. They have now been using FirstClass for seven years, but are also using WebCT, Blackboard and TopClass. Deakin has been reviewing its use of learning management systems, to consolidate online learning and get one learning management system supported centrally. Deakin Online is their strategy to get this corporate model for online learning.

Deakin also recognises the basic requirements that can be served by going online, these include meeting the needs of potential students (a promotional reason) and secondly to meet the needs of students who are off campus (providing basic information such as learning objectives, deadlines etc). Information Communication Technology (ICT) is used to enhance teaching and learning, to provide interaction and good content, its use is not efficiency driven. Deakin differentiates students when they enroll as on campus or off campus students, but they are finding that the patterns of study of on campus students are changing and that making materials available online helps reinforce this change. It provides on campus students with flexibility and choice to manage their time.

Implementation strategy: Deakin Online

The Deakin Online project has been a three year process overall and is linked to the Teaching and Learning Management Plan (TLMP). The TLMP is the driver for all these developments. The first year was consultative, from this start it has generally then focused down to actions. These have included developing policies, to drive front end developments:

- Education policy - pedagogy in an online environment.

- Strategic policy - planning tool to help people decide on the preparation of materials.

- Code of good online practice.

Deakin Online is a gateway providing access to services such as enrolment, library, administration, student life (see later) and Information Technology Support (ITS) as well as teaching and learning (schools, faculties, subjects and academics). The back end of the system is driven by two databases, Callista - student records and Oracle finance database.

The change strategy in the university has been helped by large adoption of FirstClass over the past seven years. They expect the introduction of the Deakin Online gateway to be a more significant change than earlier online learning developments. They have a Deakin Online representative in each faculty who will have responsibility for staff development and all, with the exception of the Science faculty, have employed staff locally to support developments within the faculties.

Change process to drive learning and teaching with technology will also be driven by their course accreditation process every 5 years - extensive documentation that requires them to think of learning approaches. The university has also introduced the use of portfolios as part of the academic staff promotion process.

Through Deakin Online the university is seeking to get a base line for a commonality/minimum of provision (though not in terms of teaching & learning which is under faculty control). This approach will require extensive staff development. Deakin Online is a top down initiative but in response to bottom up diverse developments. It will provide a corporate approach drawing together institutional expertise. The aim is to have 100% online by 2005 (recognising different levels of being online).

Support for learning and teaching

Learning Services (www.deakin.edu.au/learningservices/) provide support for online learning and teaching. It includes Learning Environments (online teaching and learning, educational design, AV, graphic design) and Learning Resources (copyright, materials development). Learning Services are funded centrally and consult with the faculties to identify projects and priorities. In the past the focus has been on big projects, multimedia type developments, but they envisage that in the future it will be on smaller projects. When developing online courses in the past they have not tended to build in the need for upgrades. They now recognise the need to build in evaluation intervention to see whether units need updating or improving. Emphasis will be shifting to many units; assessing appropriate use and recognising that good practice is good enough.

Learning Services do recognise the need to be more visible in the university and that is a challenge they now face. This is one of the reasons why they expect to change to working on more smaller projects so they can be more visible to more people.

Case Study – Digital Object Management Systems (DOMS)

The DOMS (Digital Object Management Systems) project is being run to set up a system to record doms in the university, and is being led by Learning Services who have consulted with faculties to find out what use they will make.

The process started six months ago to identify what is meant by doms. Drivers for this project were the amendments to the copyright act which demanded having better storage and tracking mechanism, and increased digital production. Plus they wanted to interface with the new learning management system, student records, staff, stores, finance etc and is linked with streamlining off campus provision. Also they wanted to link with digital production management system.

After consultation they came up with a specification for doms, this is being put out to tender to software providers. Expectation is to buy an off the shelf product which will require some in-house amendments. They are looking at off the shelf systems i.e. Masterfile (US) and Harvest Road, both of which have links with WebCT and Blackboard. They want to try and integrate implementation with the new learning management system.

The aim is not to have a repository, but to tag items so the university knows what is available, where it is in the university, how it is being used, and to overcome copyright issues and avoid duplication. There was discussion on the distinction between learning objects and digital objects (digital objects can be just an image for example, a learning object requires more). Started with a focus more on learning objects, but there was an expectation from the university that it would include all online material. Now, probably do mean that digital objects includes any digital object, but not all digital material in the university; focus still more toward learning objects.

There are technical issues concerning integration plus political issues. These include the management and ownership of the digital objects and the willingness to share. Change and personal issues are big, how open do academics want the system to be? Will objects be allowed to be changed? What is shareable and what is not? May look at having restricted access in some cases. (For example, copyright law exempts disabled students - so they will be able to digitise information for them but so that it is only be accessible to them). There are also issues as to how doms will be accessed, they had anticipated delivery via learning management systems or library catalogue and some are suggesting students should have direct access to doms.

Deakin may look to collaborate with other institutions also developing metadata. Practicalities of coming up with and maintaining consistent thesaurus of their own for metadata will be huge! Nightmare scenario and to train academics.

Another issue is the digital production management system and to have this integrated. Want this system to track development of materials and be able to identify progress and work that developers are doing on projects.

Staff development

Staff development for Flexible learning: 'Teaching and Learning at Deakin University: a guide to development and delivery' was a 180 pages guide to 'the challenge of investigating and adopting contemporary teaching and learning practices'. The university is currently evaluating the appropriateness for mainstream use of a seven-module online training program to develop, in staff and students, the competencies required for obtaining an International Computer Driver's Licence. Support for FirstClass is provided via FirstClass conferences.

The change process to drive learning and teaching with technology will also be driven by their course accreditation process every 5 years - extensive documentation that requires them to think of learning approaches. The university has also introduced the use of portfolios as part of the academic staff promotion process.

Deakin Online is also helping to give a more institutional focus through a central Human Resource unit that offers generic staff development including IT. Academic staff development is delegated to each faculty and each faculty deals with this differently and it can be delegated to schools. Each faculty has a member of staff responsible for online developments, and all except the Science faculty, have employed staff locally to support developments within the faculties. Deakin Online has made it easier to run staff development between faculties. Prior to this the structure forced an internal faculty focus.

Student support

The Deakin learning toolkit (DLT) is a 2 CD resource that each student is given when starting at Deakin. One CD provides the software that the students need, in addition they are given a book on using FirstClass. The second CD includes orientation videos, library, study skills, essay writing guide and ITS support information. The Student Life unit also has 14 different conferences in FirstClass on topics such as exam preparation, orientation, remote and overseas students, support resources and careers.

Library

Deakin believe their library provision for distance education is the best in the world. It is an important asset in terms of business for the university for both research and taught courses. They post books around the world and pay for students to return them.

Learning Services are investigating digital printing on demand so that students can select articles they require from a reading list, rather than be sent a complete pack. This is work in progress in Australia but DeakinPrime have links with some print shops in the USA where they can print locally but charges go to Deakin (which saves postage and delivery time). As developers, Learning Services want to send out materials as required — because this supports a developmental learning approach. This is in conflict with Despatch who want one parcel per year.

Relationships

DeakinPrime is one of Australia's largest providers of professional education, training and employee development services with more than 60,000 participants enrolled in programs throughout the world. As the corporate arm of Deakin University, DeakinPrime provides corporations, industry, government, unions and professional associations with accessible and effective modes of training for their workplace learners.

Deakin International
(www.deakin.edu.au/international) is the focal
point for Deakin University's international
activities and drives the university's international
strategic direction through promotion of the
university's profile and activities internationally,
management of the flow of students into and out
of Australia, facilitation of the delivery of the
university's expertise internationally and the
reporting of the consequences of these
international activities to the university

Analysis and emerging themes

- Deakin is, in its own and others, opinion, one
  of the leading universities in the adoption of
  ICT in the learning process. Landmarks are
  the huge number of international students.

- It has, like many others, a special group
  devoted to ICT-driven innovations in learning,
  which carries out pilot projects. The internal
  campus-wide dissemination of the results
  however is not always optimal.

- Like any university there is a struggle (or
  cross fertilisation) between the top down and
  bottom up approach: Deakin Online is an
  example of the first; the diverse faculty
  initiatives of the second.

- Deakin now faces a major challenge: the
  choice and implementation of a new digital
  learning environment combined with a
  further expansion of Deakin Online to a
  portal and DOMS (a knowledge
  management system).

Recommended web-links

Faculty of Arts
www.deakin.edu.au/fac_arts/faculty/

Diwurruwurru web site
http://arts.deakin.edu.au/diwurruwurru/

Audio streaming
www.deakin.edu.au/streaming/

Health & Behavioural Sciences
www.hbs.deakin.edu.au/faculty/

Deakin Faculty of Education
www.deakin.edu.au/faculty/

Doctoral studies online
http://education.deakin.edu.au/dso/

Learning Services
www.deakin.edu.au/learningservices/

Deakin International comprises:

- Deakin International Executive
**www.deakin.edu.au/visitors/about/DI_
Exec_Jul01.doc**

- Corporate Services Division
**www.deakin.edu.au/visitors/about/
Corporate_Serv_00.doc**

- International Recruitment Division
**www.deakin.edu.au/visitors/about/
IRD_Jul01.doc**

- International Student Support Division
**www.deakin.edu.au/visitors/about/
Int_St_Supp_Div.doc**

- Deakin University English Language Institute
**www.deakin.edu.au/visitors/about/
DUELI_structure_Jul01.doc**

- Education Abroad Office
**www.deakin.edu.au/visitors/about/
Edu_Abroad_Office_Jul01.doc**

1. Perspective on e-Learning in Australia

Barbara Watson

Overview and aims of the perspective

This perspective focuses on e-learning in the Australian universities visited by the ALT/SURF group. First, there is an overview of the major pedagogical basis for e-learning. This is followed by an overview of the extent to which e-learning is used for distance learning. The section on learning environments identifies the extent to which they have been implemented across campus, policies regarding academic ownership and content creation and some evaluations. A summary of innovations relates to more detailed descriptions given in the visit reports. The methods of dissemination are considered and information about some research into e-learning.

E-learning is an important part of higher education in Australia. During 2001 a survey was undertaken by the Australian Department of Education, Science and Training (DEST) to ascertain the current extent of online education in Australian universities (Bell, 2002). The survey distinguishes between online courses, units and services. Online courses are defined as 'university award courses in which all units or subjects are delivered and all interactions between staff and students are conducted via the Internet.' The survey found 207 online courses delivered by 23 Australian universities, of which 90% are at postgraduate level. Online units are defined as 'subjects or course components, in which at least some of the content is delivered and/or some of the interaction is conducted via the Internet.' Online participation in these units is divided into 3 categories:

- Web - supplemented – optional (46%).

- Web - dependent – compulsory (54%).

- Fully online – no face to face component (1.4%).

The survey found that all universities are using the web to some extent for teaching and learning. However, this had a large range from 99-100% in 7 universities to 9% in one university.

Pedagogies

The major pedagogies underlying e-learning in Australia are flexible learning and constructivism. Problem-based learning is used extensively in Medicine, for example, at Monash and Melbourne. The motives behind using these pedagogies are both a desire to increase the quality of learning and teaching and commercial.

There is a difference between flexible learning and flexible provision. The Australian Evaluation and Investigations Programme (EIP) study of 'The Effectiveness of Models of Flexible Provision of Higher Education' found a wide range of approaches to the flexible provision of HE and in many universities several approaches co-existed. The EIP study distinguished the following categories and strategies of flexible provision on the basis of literature and responses to the survey:

'Provision affording access and convenience:

- Moving time and place of study to suit the learner.

- Removing fixed time and place constraints.

- Removing entry requirements.

Provision accommodating learning preferences:

- Providing alternative entry and exit points;

- Accommodating learning style, pace and collaboration preferences;

- Accommodating content and assessment preferences' (Ling, 2001).

In this study the use of new learning technologies to address the quality of learning did not come within the definition of flexible provision but the practices that arose from it were included.

Collis identifies 'four key components of flexible learning - technology, pedagogy, implementation strategies and institutional framework' (Collis, 2001). The key idea being 'learner choice in different aspects of the learning experience.' She defines the possibilities for flexible provision in terms of five dimensions – time, content, entry requirements, instructional approach and resources, and delivery and logistics. These dimensions are similar to the categories defined by the EIP study.

One of the factors influencing greater flexibility is the changing student profile with more 'learner-earner' (i.e. the full time student who also has a paid job), and 'earner-learners' (i.e. people with a full time job, who undertake study) (Bell, 2002). Students are trying to cope with the demands of both work and study and so need more flexible forms of education. E-learning can enable flexible learning and greater flexibility.

The other main pedagogic influence in Australia is constructivism. There are many definitions of constructivism. Tait suggests that they are derived from some common principles, which he summarises as:

- 'learning involves the active construction of a personal conceptual knowledge base by the learner;

- learning is reflective and builds on and also develops the learner's existing knowledge;

- learning benefits from views of the subject area;

- learning is facilitated by authentic activity relevant to the situation in which it will be applied' (Tait 1997).

Flexible learning is an important part of the strategies and mission statements of many of the universities visited. E-learning is the main method used to increase flexible learning.

The mission of Southern Cross University (SCU) stresses flexible learning. Their prime focus in setting up flexible learning is to attain quality, not the enrolment of large amounts of new students. This concept is the central argument in choosing e-learning and online solutions and affects nearly all other strategic and educational decisions. Since 1996 senior management of the university have stressed and pushed the use of online provisions in the educational design of all the courses as a particular interpretation of the concept of flexible learning. This central directive was, to a certain extent in conflict with very different interpretations of the concept by educational designers and academic staff.

Similarly, the philosophy of the University of Melbourne is to make face-to-face education more flexible by using e-learning. The university sees e-learning as a way of improving the quality of teaching, expanding its student base and generating income through internationalisation. The use of e-learning in teaching may be a means of handling large class groups while maintaining or improving teaching quality, and only incidentally as an efficiency measure. The focus is, notably, on multimedia, with general consideration of the use of the Internet and the Web in teaching starting to emerge. This university states that it will be a front-runner in e-learning in education. Building on the strategic plan, the university aims at 70% of academic staff in each department to be using multimedia in their teaching and that the proportion of students responding positively to use of multimedia should be not less than 70%. There is no generic guiding model that drives the e-learning-related activities as the university respects the autonomy of the academic staff. It is the individual academic that generates the idea and drives that implementation. Most projects reflect a very student-centred approach. Internationalisation, through participating in Universitas 21, is seen as a means of positioning the university in the forefront of emerging learning technologies, environments and pedagogies, as well as generating revenue to re-invest in their campus environments.

Deakin University is also using e-learning to enhance teaching and learning, rather than to increase efficiency. It is committed to offering flexible study opportunities and courses are available on and off campus and through full and part-time study or a combination of modes. To assist students studying away from the campuses the university provides high quality print, audio, computer and video materials. The process of going online is making academics think about the pedagogy of their course.

At the Griffith University, flexible learning is one of the five areas identified for strategic development (Griffith, 1999). Flexible learning is defined as student-centred with the academic acting as facilitator, away from the traditional model of teaching, involving deep learning and using online components. Logan was the first campus to try flexible learning in a corporate way with the intention to replicate this at other campuses (Ling, P, 2001).

Flexibility and student-centred learning are the two main themes in learning and teaching that are promoted within Monash. Flexibility is used to enable Monash to target different groups with different needs. For example, undergraduates and lawyers in continuing education are both served, but using completely different formats. Monash offers different combinations of on campus, hybrid and fully online programs and subjects. The university wants to provide learning flexibility without it being burdensome to the institution. The aim is to use technology to enable student-centred flexible learning and not to drive it.

The mission of University of Southern Queensland (USQ) is to be a leader in international and distance education. Professor P. Swannell, the Vice-Chancellor, has stated that, 'the important characteristic of a successful e-university is that it surrounds its people with the best possible technology, implementing the best possible pedagogy.' He states that people are of central importance to the educational process supported by the high quality, carefully designed and delivered study materials. Central to the constructivist philosophy of online teaching and learning at USQ is what they describe as 'the creation of communities of practice'. The rationale is to create the collaborative, reflective practitioner through the intelligent use of online group work facilitated by an online tutor.

Queens University of Technology's (QUT) strategic priorities for learning and teaching are:

- Generic graduate capabilities;

- Flexible learning technologies;

- Improving assessment;

- indigenous perspectives in the curriculum;

- Internationalisation of the curriculum.

QUT encourages scholarly activity and the scholarship of teaching. Scholarly activity is ensuring that your teaching is informed by scholarship. The scholarship of teaching is about researching the teaching of your subject, or scholarly teaching plus reflection on what you are doing. The instructional design model used is basically 'social constructivist.

Charles Sturt University (CSU) is shifting emphasis from teaching to learning and a move from dual-mode to multi-mode learning (on campus, partnerships, workplace-based learning, distributed education, and access centres). Similarly, the main pedagogical principle at University of Technology Sydney (UTS) is flexible learning, which is defined variously from merely studying outside office hours to problem-based learning.

Flexible learning and constructivism are the main pedagogies in the Australian universities which were visited. E-learning is the main method of enabling flexible learning.

Distance Learning

The 'Business for Borderless Education' international study examined the activities of corporate, virtual and for-profit organisations. It found a 'rapid growth of technology-based distance education in a market traditionally strongly dominated by campus-based education.' (Cunningham, 2000)

Australia has a 'strong tradition of distance learning, due to our small population and vast geographical distances' (Bell, 2001). Therefore it is not surprising that in higher education some universities, such as USQ, CSU, Deakin, Murdoch and Monash, have a high commitment to distance learning. This commitment is often based in the historical development of their institution. Surprisingly, the distance learning

often uses traditional modes of delivery and includes little e-learning. There are different methods of supporting distance learning and these include the development of campuses in other countries and companies and forming overseas partnerships. Some universities, such as Melbourne and Wollongong, have decided to concentrate on campus education and have very little distance learning.

Changing technology

The use of technology in distance learning is changing. According to Professor James Taylor (USQ) distance education has evolved through four distinct phases:

1. The correspondence model – print based.

2. The multi-media model – print, audio and video technologies utilised.

3. The tele-learning model – based on applications of telecommunication technologies (allows synchronous communication).

4. The flexible learning model – based on online delivery via the internet.

He suggests that a fifth generation of distance learning is emerging, which he calls the 'Intelligent Flexible Learning Model'. While essentially a derivation of the fourth generation, the fifth generation aims to capitalise on the opportunities provided by the development of the Internet and the WWW. Taylor's model would automate most interaction between student and teacher/institution, and thus reduce the variable costs associated with increasing student numbers, whether on or off campus. A tenfold productivity will be achieved from student tutor ratios of 20:1 to 200:1. (Taylor, 2001)

USQ has been involved in distance education since 1977 when it commenced implementing dual-mode programmes. The Australian Federal Government has designated USQ a National Distance Education Centre and has provided a capital investment grant of AU$10 million to enable the provision of a 'state of the art infrastructure for flexible delivery technologies'. USQ has a reputation as an international leader in online and distance learning aiming to provide flexible study choice to students through on campus, off campus and online options. Almost three-quarters of all students are directly involved in distance programmes. In 2001 there were about 5,000 on campus students and nearly 16,000 external students from over 60 countries. Forty-five of those countries have online learning facilities and only 15 are mixed-mode (print, CDs, audio). Online learning is recognised as being very resource intensive with class sizes being reduced to 20 – 30 students. Most online students are postgraduate and have learned the skills of studying independently so the Virtual School project is investigating whether younger learners can study effectively online. Some academics still prefer the face-to-face environment, but many are teaching a mix of face-to-face and distance education. USQ stills wants to retain on campus education as well as distance learning.

The mission of Charles Sturt University (CSU) has historically involved the delivery of higher education through distance education both nationally and internationally. This has led to an early commitment to the use of e-learning in programme delivery and their claim to providing the most extensive online support in Australia of distance education courses. CSU currently has about 30,000 students enrolled across campuses (14,000 full time equivalents). Of these, some 22,000 are registered as distance education students of which 12,000 are from Sydney, Wollongong and Newcastle, 5,000 are from the rest of mainland Australia and 5,000 are offshore students.

Deakin University is 25 years old and was set up for distance education in Victoria with a mandate from the start for having on and off campus students and providing equity between them. Their model for distance education was adopted from the Open University with the use of course teams to develop materials and there has always been a focus on technology even with the initial audio visual and print materials. Many courses were developed for distance education first and then transferred to on campus delivery. This has led to a culture that makes it easier to adopt new technologies into teaching and learning.

Murdoch has a long history of distance learning. The focus has shifted from the delivery of materials, such as audiotapes of lectures, to access to materials. Some Murdoch Online external units may require on campus attendance for laboratory practicals or other specialised purposes

Providing local support

Monash has a different approach to distance learning as it not only has a number of campuses in the Melbourne area, but also in Malaysia and Southern Africa. Furthermore centres are opened in the UK, Italy and Germany. About 50,000 students are enrolled in a wide variety of programmes. This number includes 11,000 off campus students. Distance students are served by a combination of paper-based materials, CD-ROMs and online support. Fully online modules may opt for some face-to-face options.

Southern Cross University (SCU) also has a distinct approach to distance education based on overseas partnerships. Students enroll in local institutions and take courses, which generally involve face-to-face meetings with local tutors and print-based materials. To guarantee quality, 20% to 100% of the assessment is controlled by SCU and the students receive SCU certificates. This approach is reflected in the way learning materials are being developed as flexible and re-usable.

Campus-based

Some universities have little interest in distance education. For example, Wollongong is not a distance learning university. However, it received funding for a postgraduate education project (PAGE) to help set up structures to support distance learning, as it was recognised that the university was faced with a changing student population. Its distance learning courses can be online or include a hybrid approach making use of both CD-ROM and Internet. At the University of Melbourne there is only distance education in a few specific areas, such as Agriculture and Education, which have campuses outside the metropolitan area. Similarly, QUT is a campus-based university, which emphasises the experience that students have by being there. It also has some distance education in Education. QUT anticipates that notions of campus-based and distance learning will become meaningless, as a new paradigm will enter.

E-learning is becoming part of distance learning in Australia as technologies change. The main issues facing distance learning concern supporting distance learners, student skills in online learning and academic attitudes and experiences. The distinction between on campus and distance students is becoming blurred as more students are living locally but taking 'distance' modules.

Learning Environments (LEs)

Most Australian universities have selected a learning environment (LE) for their learning and teaching. This LE may be part of a managed learning environment (MLE) and/or linked to their university portal. The majority have chosen a commercial LE, with Blackboard (17 universities) and WebCT (29 universities) sharing the market (Bell, 2002). Twenty universities have developed their own in-house system. Some universities are using several systems as the DEST survey into Online Education collected data from 40 out of the 43 Australian universities and the total number of LEs is 66. Table 4 refers to the universities visited and give details of the software, extent of use and URL of the University portal or LE.

Most of these portals and LEs have been given names which relate to, and identify, the institution. This personalises the portal/LE for the user and makes them feel part of the institution.

At most universities the implementation of the LEs is mainly still at the pilot stage within faculties and is not yet campus wide. The key issues concerning the implementation are academic ownership, the development of the content, staff support and development within a changing culture. There has been little evaluation of the effect of LEs on student learning.

University	Name	Software	URL
Charles Sturt (CSU)	myCSU	Own Considering Blackboard	my.csu.edu.au
Deakin	Deakin Online	Currently, FirstClass and Topclass Choosing between BB and WebCT	www.deakin.edu.au/deakinonline
Edith Cowan (ECU)	MyECU	Blackboard	http://MyECU.ecu.edu.au
Griffith – Logan	Learning@GU	Blackboard	www2.gu.edu.au/
Melbourne		Moving to WebCT	http://webraft.its.unimelb.edu.au/
Monash		WebCT and own	https://my.monash.edu.au/
Murdoch	Murdoch Online	WebCT	www.murdoch.edu.au/online/
Queensland University of Technology (QUT)	QUTVirtual OLT	Variety of tools	https://qutvirtual.qut.edu.au/ https://olt.qut.edu.au/
Southern Cross (SCU)	MySCU	Blackboard	http://study.scu.edu.au
University Southern Queensland (USQ)	USQOnline	NextEd (with Blackboard) and WebCT	www.usqonline.com.au/
University Technology Sydney (UTS)		Blackboard	http://online.uts.edu.au/
University Western Australia (UWA)		WebCT	
West One		WebCT	
Wollongong		WebCT	www.uow.edu.au/LOL/

Table 4 – LEs/portals in Australia

Implementation stage

Since July 2000, SCU has been one of the few universities that has all of its students online. Its current approach builds on a slow start up phase. Initially, Learning Space was adopted but the uptake was poor. A review of available solutions on the e-learning market focused on finding a transparent system and BlackBoard was adopted.

QUT also has a campus wide LE which uses its own in-house system called OLT (Online Teaching). OLT is a support process offering a wide range of services to students from timetables to learning materials. Access to timetables prior to enrolment enables students to organise their studies and work commitments.

Murdoch Online is the university's coordinated approach to using the Internet for teaching and learning. Units which are online have Internet-based delivery as an essential requirement and are in two main forms according to students' needs and circumstances:

1. Online external–campus attendance not required.

2. Online internal–integrated with weekly classes.

Nearly all units are based upon the WebCT environment and therefore typically include study guides, materials, web links, discussion groups and assignments.

With the introduction of electronic delivery, CSU's Vice-Chancellor required an electronic forum to be set up for all subjects. In principle, this provides a means of interaction between all students on a given course and their lecturers.

Deakin University aims to be 100% online by 2005 due to a management-led initiative. It currently uses Firstclass and is now choosing between WebCT and Blackboard for Deakin Online. There have been problems with getting campus students to work online as they want face-to-face teaching. Consequently, online learning has been promoted as a new skill for prospective employers. Students are not given an introduction to working online although there are 'occasional lifelines'. The Virtual Learning Environment is used for collaborative work through exchange of documents and individual students are given specific roles within groups such as chairing and maintaining documents.

Some universities have not yet implemented an LE across their institution. The University of Melbourne is planning the introduction of WebCT following a survey of user needs, but it will not be mandatory to use it. Edith Cowan introduced Blackboard in February 2002 and has found that it has been speedily taken up by academics. Modules are categorised into mode A (web supplemental), mode B (web dependent) or mode C (fully online) and mode B is encouraged. Blackboard training is compulsory. At Griffith the priority is to develop flexible subjects and full programmes which can be used at several campuses.

Some universities are supporting more than one LE. Monash supports both WebCT and an in-house system, which it hopes to integrate this into its new portal. The new portal is designed to provide 'a virtual gateway to support student centred flexible learning by coordinating many of the university's key resources to meet the needs of students and staff.' (Kennedy, 2002)

USQ are also using two LEs. USQ has interesting partnerships with commercial companies to provide an LE for their distance learners. USQ Online uses Blackboard as a platform and has been created in collaboration with NextEd. NextEd negotiate with Blackboard over global changes to the system in order to customise Blackboard for USQ. NextEd hosts server sites in appropriate global locations and provides 24 hour online support. The other LE is WebCT which is used for on campus students. There is some concern that undergraduates, especially school leavers, may not have acquired the necessary pattern of independent learning skills required for learning successfully online. Most of the online learning programmes are in the Faculties of Education and Business.

Academic ownership

Some universities support academic ownership of their LEs by creating any online course which is requested and by enabling academics to upload materials directly. Others are more restrictive and will only accept requests for courses and content upload via a third party.

Wollongong has the policy that requests for sites are only accepted through subject co-ordinators, who have had WebCT training. The process of WebCT site creation starts with a subject co-ordinator speaking to an educational developer. The subject co-ordinator then completes a web-based request form. At USQ academics have little control as the units are prepared by the learning support team working with the academics and the completed units are delivered to NextEd to mount on the Blackboard system.

At QUT academic control over content was a prime consideration. This was their reason for not purchasing Blackboard or WebCT, and setting up a 'more flexible approach' in which a number of different tools are connected via a web framework. The pedagogy was designed around the use of the tools. However, Education faculty members at QUT do not feel that they have ownership of their LE as they have to contact central support to have any changes implemented. They also feel that there is a cultural gap between instructional designers from central support who have never taught giving advice to an Education faculty. Consequently, staff members are providing peer support to help their colleagues with online learning.

Content

The universities have different approaches to providing online content and there is much debate about the pedagogical value of placing lecture notes online

CSU has approximately 2500 courses so it was not feasible to convert all their paper-based materials into online learning activities. Therefore, pre-existing paper-based materials were scanned and made available electronically alongside the printed materials. New courses are developed electronically first and a printed version can be produced from them.

At SCU, academics who had web sites before Blackboard was adopted, are encouraged to integrate them into their Blackboard courses. Sharing and reuse of materials within schools is encouraged at Griffith, which has a strong emphasis on providing multimedia content as part of its flexible learning resources.

Evaluation

Surprisingly, there has been little evaluation of the effect of LEs on learning and teaching. The evaluations, which have been carried out, have usually been of the form of surveys and user statistics and have often been undertaken by central support services.

At CSU an evaluation of the electronic forums, which were set up for all subjects, was undertaken about three years after implementation. This study showed that less than 10% of these forums were being used for 'good' educational purposes and 70% were not being used at all. Their conclusions from evaluating this experience are:

- Content is good but communication is everything.

- Scalability is everything.

- Nothing scales like automation.

However they have no data about the impact on students' learning.

At Wollongong a staff survey is going to be undertaken on an annual basis, which will aim to find out what tools are being used and to show the level and pattern of use. Results so far show that WebCT is being used for a wide range and increasing number of functions. Feedback also suggests that it is becoming fundamental to the running of courses.

Student feedback at Deakin is mixed as some students are very positive, but others do not want to participate in online learning. At QUT some evaluation is undertaken by the central support service. An instructional designer works with an academic to decide what to evaluate and the most appropriate methodology. However, QUTVirtual is a portal rather than a teaching tool so there have been few educational changes.

USQ is evaluating the performance of online learning by analysing the statistics that are automatically generated on the number of hits per student in areas such as content and communication.

Learning environments are being used to support e-learning in many Australian universities. This is mainly still at a pilot stage within faculties and raising issues of academic ownership and content development. The impact on student learning has generally not been evaluated beyond obtaining user statistics.

Innovations

There are many innovative projects being undertaken at Australian universities. Table 5 summarises case studies of innovations that are described in detail in the other chapters.

Evaluation

The situation regarding the evaluation of innovations is similar to the evaluation of the use of learning environments. There has been limited evaluation of the innovative projects. In some cases the evaluation has been obtained through

Project title	University	Brief description
	Melbourne	Showcase examples www.infodiv.unimelb.edu.au/telars/cds/services/gdprojshowcase.shtml
Digital Object Management Systems (DOMS)	Deakin	Aim to tag DOMS so that the university knows what is available, where it is and how it is being used.
Digital portfolio	Edith Cowan	The development of a digital portfolio system to be used by students for reflection and study planning.
Flexible Pedagogies Initiative		Exploring and developing aspects of flexibility http://education.qut.edu.au/fo/fpi/fpihomebase.html
iLectures	University of Western Australian	Audio recordings with PowerPoint slides of 150 lectures a week available within 3 hours of the lecture (http://ilectures.uwa.edu.au)
South coast arts	Wollongong	Development of provision to outreach centres
USQAssist	University of Southern Queensland	The automated project builds on previous knowledge creating an increasingly populating database of answers to queries

Table 5 – Summary of innovations

the process of obtaining student feedback on courses. However, in some universities, academics are not required to evaluate their teaching. The evaluation is often undertaken by central services.

At Deakin University the focus has been on a few large innovative projects with multimedia developments, but it is envisaged that in the future there will be more smaller projects. This idea may be developed to the extent of offering each individual academic one hour with an educational developer to discuss potential ideas for online learning. Evaluation will become part of the project development to assess appropriate use and the need for further updates or improvements. An example of project evaluation was undertaken by central Learning Services for the Education Online course. This course was developed in the late 90s as a stand-alone environment to access resources and activities for the undergraduate on campus students. The evaluation found that a major issue was professional development for staff. The impact of this course on student learning has not been evaluated because of the difficulties in measuring it and relating the finding to previous years.

At Griffith the Logan campus was planned and constructed as a flexible learning environment. However, many of the initial team of academics and instructional designers have left because they could not sustain enthusiasm in the face of administrative frustrations. Their model of flexible learning was not sustainable as it was too expensive in staff time, so courses have now changed back to a more traditional mode. It also could not be repeated elsewhere because of different teaching cultures.

At QUT, units are evaluated at least once every five years. There is a performance development review but academics are not required to evaluate their teaching. At SCU, a Student

Feedback System has been developed, which is not mandatory but is used by about two-thirds of the staff. It is the intention at Wollongong to carry out an audit of how e-learning is used within their institution. It is recognised that it is still mainly text-based information delivery with few multimedia or collaborative learning developments. An online survey tool has been developed which enables lecturers to create their own questions or to select them from a database. This system provides a quick way for lecturers to receive feedback. Wollongong have found that online surveys have a lower return but the data is much richer.

The central services at the University of Melbourne support academics in evaluating the effectiveness of integrating technology into their teaching. Similarly, at Monash, the evaluation research includes subject evaluation, research into student experiences, employer satisfaction surveys and expert evaluations of graduates and postgraduate programs.

Some central services have developed an evaluation framework for academics to use. For example, Murdoch University coordinates a national project about a learner-centred evaluation framework (LCE). This has been developed to help academics and research staff evaluate e-learning projects. However, the cost of the LCE is prohibitive at AU$15,000 dollars for each evaluation project.

The Department of Teaching, Learning and Research Support (TeLaRS) at University of Melbourne is starting a major research project which aims to investigate:

1. How the use of information and communications technology (ICT) is influencing teaching practices at the University of Melbourne

2. How are students' approaches to learning being modified by the use of ICT in a campus-based educational environment?

(www.infodiv.unimelb.edu.au/telars/re/ ret.html)

Another idea for evaluation is Taylor's construction of a national scheme for external peer review of ICT-based teaching and learning resources, which may have a trial implementation in future (Taylor, 2001).

The evaluations have resulted in some universities deciding to support more small scale innovations rather than a few large ones, recognising the need for more staff development and the problems of scalability of projects. Course evaluation is not compulsory in all universities and some evaluation methodology is too expensive for widespread adoption.

Research

Some universities are researching into e-learning and this research is being undertaken through specialist units, Learning and Teaching Support Units as well as through the faculties of Education.

At the University of Wollongong specialist units called the Research Centre for Interactive Learning Environments (RILE) and the Digital Media Centre (DMC) involve academics and postgraduates in research. Their research has identified key principles for quality designs for online learning and identified four reusable learning design templates.

At the University of Melbourne the Centre for the Study of Higher Education (CSHE) is a national and international leader in higher education policy research and educational development (www.cshe.unimelb.edu.au/). For more than 30 years CSHE has provided independent, research-based advice and support on matters of teaching and learning, the student experience, professional development for academics, and quality assurance policies and processes. The Centre undertakes research projects for the state and federal governments. To foster the adoption of e-learning, there is a strong focus on setting up research about the e-learning-related projects to research their impact. This is considered as important for adoption by academic staff in a research-led institution.

At the University of Western Australian (UWA) there is strong evidence of growing interest into research in teaching and learning during academic year 2001/2002. During that time period the Centre for the Advancement of Teaching and Learning (CATL) awarded two major grants of AU$50,000 and AU$40,000 respectively plus a further ten grants of approximately AU$10,000 each (www.catl.uwa.edu.au/).

Taylor's research into online group work has suggested that there are three major patterns of performance. The first two categories, workers and lurkers while operating in different ways, do participate equally. The third category, sleepers, do not seem to be engaging with the group learning process. The quality of the interactions appears to be improved when students make statements which are peer reviewed. The reason for this could be because they challenge each other's ideas and so raise the standard of interactions. (Taylor, 2001)

The Universities Online survey recommends that 'further research and evaluation of learning processes and learning outcomes associated with flexible provision of higher education is required.' (Bell, 2002).

Dissemination

There are limited mechanisms for the dissemination of e-learning experiences within and between Australian universities compared to the UK and the Netherlands. One of the reasons for this is that there is no equivalent of the UK Learning and Teaching Support Network (LTSN) and the SURF Foundation in the Netherlands. Within institutions most dissemination activities are carried out within faculties, although some university-wide dissemination may be the responsibility of institutional learning and teaching support units. The mechanisms for dissemination range from web pages, mailing lists and databases to seminars and conferences.

An example of dissemination within a faculty is the teaching and learning festival in the Faculty of Arts at Deakin University. This festival provided hands-on workshops and seminars in which academics talked about their use of technology.

Dissemination across faculties is encouraged at UTS through Flexible Learning Action Groups (FLAG). They meet regularly and discuss pedagogical and technical issues, based on own experiences on e-learning in education, and this enables the exchange of good practice. However, at the University of Melbourne, the lunchtime seminars run by the Department of Teaching, Learning and Research Support (TeLaRS) were not well attended. At QUT there is an annual teaching conference at which 'Compassionate Pioneer awards' are presented to those who have helped others get online. Both students and staff can nominate individuals.

Conclusion

The Australian universities, which were visited, are at a similar stage as the Netherlands and the UK in the development of e-learning and

implementation of LEs. E-learning is mainly based on flexible learning and constructivism. Most universities have selected an LE, but few have implemented it across the whole university. There are different policies towards academic ownership and creation of content within the LEs. There has been little evaluation of the effect of an LE on learning and teaching. The evaluation of other e-learning innovations is either very extensive and expensive, or nearly non-existent. There are varying levels of dissemination of the results of these evaluations and research. Some universities have internal mechanisms for dissemination across the university. At others dissemination is mainly within faculties. There is no equivalent of the UK's Learning and Teaching Support Network (LTSN) and the Dutch SURF Foundation to disseminate across universities.

Some universities have a strong commitment to distance learning with many overseas students. However, the division between on campus and distance learning is becoming blurred as more local students choose to be distant learners to gain flexibility in their studies. This distance learning is often based on traditional methodology with little e-learning, although it may use an LE.

The Universities Online study found that the provision of online learning depended on 'the philosophy of the university and/or the enthusiasm of individual staff members' (Bell, 2002). The study concludes that Australian universities are embracing the concept of online learning as 54% contain online components. The percentage of web supplemented units shows that many institutions are using online teaching to add value to teaching and learning.

Acknowledgments

Jill Armstrong, Petra Boezerooy, Betty Collis, Bas Cordewener, Janet Hanson, Robert Harding, Arthur Loughran, Helen McEvoy, Marcel Miranda, Wiebe Nijlunsing, Rhonda Riachi, Annette Roeters, Jan van der Veen, Martin Valcke.

References

Bell, M., Bush, D., Nicholson, P., O'Brien, D., Tran, T. 2002. Universities Online: a Survey of Online Education and Services in Australia, Occasional Paper Series 02-A, Commonwealth of Australia, 2002,
www.dest.gov.au/highered/occpaper/02a/ 02_a.pdf

Collis, B. 2001. Flexible Learning in a Digital World, Kogan Page

Cunningham, S., Ryan, Y., Stedman, L., Tapsall, S., Bagdon., Flew, T., Coaldrake, P. 2000. The Business of Borderless Education, Evaluations and Investigations Programme, Commonwealth of Australia.

Griffith University, Guidelines for Faculty Teaching and Learning Management Plans 1999 – 2001,
www.gu.edu.au:80/ua/aa/tal/tlmp/ TL_Guidelines_1999_2001.html

Kennedy, D., Webster, L., Benson, R., James, D. and Bailey, N. 2002. My.monash: Supporting Students and Staff in Teaching, Learning and Administration, Australian Journal of Educational Technology, 2002, 18(1), 24-39.
www.ascilite.org.au/ajet/ajet18/res/ kennedy.html

Ling, P., Arger, G., Smallwood, H., Toomey, R., Kirkpatrick, D., Barnard, I., 2001. The Effectiveness of Models of Flexible Provision of Higher Education, EIP Report 01/09,
www.detya.gov.au/highered/eippubs/ eip01_9/eip01_9.pdf

Tait, B., 1997. Constructive Internet based learning, Active Learning 7: 3-8, 1997

Taylor, James C. 2001. Fifth Generation Distance Education,
www.detya.gov.au/highered/hes/hes40/ hes40.pdf

Taylor, P. and Richardson, A. 2001. Validating Scholarship in University Teaching:

Constructing a National Scheme for External Peer Review of ICT-based Teaching and Learning Resources, EIP Report 01/3
www.detya.gov.au/highered/eippubs/ eip01_3/01_3.pdf

Universities Online: a Survey of Online Education and Services in Australia
www.dest.gov.au/highered/occpaper/02a/ default.htm

2. Perspective on the strategic implementation of e-Learning in Australian universities

Janet Hanson

Overview and aims of the perspective

The focus of this perspective is the strategic implementation of e-learning within the universities visited. It begins with a brief description of the factors affecting strategic planning in Australian higher education and the impact these are having on universities. It then follows an examination of the rationale for the development of e-learning with reference to these pressures. In the light of this, an analysis of the manner in which the strategic implementation is being managed is provided. This covers issues as follows:

- The role of senior management, university committees and top-down instigation of innovation through budget allocation.

- The organisation of central support services, both technical and pedagogic, and links with faculties and other support services.

- Staff developments opportunities.

- Reward and recognition for teaching or involvement in e-learning.

Factors contributing to greater use of e-Learning in Australian universities

Factors contributing to changing views about the purpose and nature of Australian universities, and therefore the context in which greater use of e-learning is situated, are similar to those affecting higher education in the UK and the Netherlands. Senior managers whom we met frequently set the context for their use of e-learning with reference to these external, shaping forces.

The first of these is the broad political drive by governments to harness higher education to the needs of the economy. Through widening access to higher education and by promoting the concept of lifelong learning, more people are being attracted to higher education who would not traditionally have considered going to university. This changing concept of seeing a degree as a route to a job has led to many changes to the curriculum, including the incorporation of vocational and transferable skills (Coaldrake and Steadman, 1999, p3).

The resulting increase in student numbers and the growth in diversity of the student population, are additional factors encouraging universities to consider new patterns of curriculum design and more flexible strategies for learning and teaching. These are aimed at increasing flexibility of access from locations other than the traditional campus, for example, from home and from the work-place. This greater diversity of student background is also resulting in the need to make changes to student support and guidance structures and processes. Students enter university with less well-developed study habits, needing a wider range of study and language support. Curricula that reflect international diversity and the need to develop the concept of global citizenship are being designed (Martin, 1999, p12).

However, as the numbers of students entering higher education has risen, so have the costs, but the corresponding per capita funding from government has not kept pace, so universities are seeking more efficient ways to deliver education and are also seeking to generate income from other sources, for example, from business enterprise. The higher fees contributed by international students, either on campus or in their home location, have become an important source of income, but this, together with home students contributing more to their fees, is resulting in a growing emphasis on customer orientation in universities (Coaldrake and Steadman, 1999, p4).

Students are but one group of a rising number of stakeholders demanding greater accountability from universities (Watson, 2000, p18). We observed the impact of this in many places, where there was evidence of careful consideration being given to strategic planning and to the challenge presented by a national quality audit system, which was a relatively recent introduction for Australian higher education.

The knowledge explosion and the ability of organisations other than universities to become global providers of higher education using information and communication technologies (ICT) was also a driver for change. ICT was posing a threat to universities as well as offering a way to meet some of the other pressures. This was reflected in the range of reasons provided for adopting e-learning within the universities we visited.

As might be expected, the established providers of distance education, for example, Deakin University and University of Southern Queensland (USQ), were making extensive use of e-learning to deliver learning materials to a wider market in Australia and elsewhere. Nevertheless, it was also being used extensively in campus-based universities such as the University of Melbourne. Some, for example, Queensland University of Technology (QUT), supported the notion that demands for greater efficiency were driving the use of e-learning, although it was recognised that it was not solely about reducing costs. Others, such as Charles Sturt University (CSU), presented evidence of the administrative

imperatives driving greater use of e-learning, and also of the importance of the regional role of the university in supporting distributed learners over a wide area. In some universities, emphasis was placed on the value of e-learning in contributing to the development of students' ICT skills in equipping them for employment. The most widely expressed over-arching reason for the greater use of e-learning was to secure greater flexibility for the students, and to enhance the quality of the student experience, whether this was campus-based or at a distance.

Several universities had entered into strategic partnerships with commercial ICT providers to develop either the technical platform, marketing opportunities, or local student support. Further details on this are provided in the section on Relationships and Partnerships. However, despite these useful links, several universities referred to the problems associated with the poor ICT infrastructure nationally, for example, bandwidth limitations, which were preventing them from increasing their use of e-learning.

Facilitating greater use of e-Learning within the Australian universities

Introduction

The generic factors affecting change in universities were seen to be having an impact on each of the universities visited in different ways. We observed a range of different approaches to establishing the structures and processes necessary for bringing about change and encouraging greater use of e-learning.

Change strategies to encourage greater use of technology for learning and teaching should take into account a number of factors. These include factors relating to organisational structures (Bates, 1997), to the individual preferences and motivations of those affected by the changes (Moore, 1991; Collis, Peters and Pals, 2000) and to the complex influence of the decentralised nature of academic culture (Bottomley et al, 1999; Coaldrake and Steadman, 1999; Taylor, 1999). This last group of authors are all commentators on the experiences of Australian universities.

Support of senior managers

Two key aspects relevant at the whole organisation level are the vision and support of the senior management, both at university and faculty level, and appropriate deliberative structures where issues relating to e-learning may be discussed, and policies agreed. As evidence of these aspects being taken into account, we were looking for strategic plans for learning and teaching, learning and teaching committees and staff in senior posts acting as 'champions' of e-learning. Most universities visited had these in place or were in the early stages of setting them up. Several universities, for example, Deakin, Melbourne, and QUT, had nominated an Assistant Dean in each of the faculties as a champion, and it was often these individuals who were members of the university learning and teaching committees. In some cases, for example, at Wollongong, faculty learning and teaching committees had been established to feed into the university level committee.

The vision for extending the use of e-learning was often expressed through a flexible learning policy. Some universities, for example, Deakin, Melbourne and University of Western Australia (UWA), had undertaken an institution-wide review of staff opinions relating to the use of ICT for learning and teaching to help with the development of the policy or to review the online platform.

Funding for e-Learning

Another key contributing factor to developing e-learning is the allocation of sufficient funds, both at an institutional level and in faculties. The creation of centrally managed strategic plans linked to budgets appeared to be a recent innovation in several universities. Prior to this, budget decisions would have been made independently at faculty level.

Universities were making funds available to promote the use of e-learning, and these ranged from large scale, faculty based projects to small scale funding of individual innovators, but it was evident that a more strategic approach was being adopted in most universities. This involved a move away from supporting individuals to supporting faculty teams.

At Melbourne, the ambitious targets in the University's Strategic Plan relating to the use of e-learning in the curriculum become realistic when the impact of a major funding scheme is considered. The 'Teaching and Learning – Multimedia and Educational Technology' (T&L(M&ET)) programme has been operating for three years, and around AU$10 million has been spent on some 218 ICT development projects. These projects had a major emphasis on multimedia initially, which, though broadly defined, tended to be interpreted as computer-aided learning resources for use by students studying at the university's campuses. Now the development of online materials is also supported. The close integration of support departments at Melbourne seems to make innovations scaleable and sustainable.

Monash has also made a large investment in this area of about AU$16 million. Quality improvement is proudly seen as a commercial selling point. On the other hand it is clear that all initiatives to innovate and increase the quality of education are balanced against the expected raise in revenues for the university.

At USQ there is funding of AU$150,000 per annum, which is allocated in sums of AU$10,000, AU$25,000 and AU$50,000. The faculty must approve project applications from individual staff before they can be put forward for a grant to ensure that the needs of the faculty are taken into consideration, as also happens at QUT.

At Deakin University, however, the focus has been on big projects involving multimedia developments, but it is envisaged that, in the future, smaller projects will be funded in order to increase the number of units online. This idea may be developed to the extent of offering each individual lecturer one hour with an educational developer to discuss potential ideas for online learning and to build in evaluation to consider need for updating.

Such an approach, using time as the currency rather than dollars and focusing on the small scale, can already be seen operating successfully at Wollongong. Here, rather than focus on whole courses, the approach taken with lecturers is to focus on 'learning objects' at the level of individual lectures or modules. The hope also is that these 'objects' can then be shared. Investigations are being undertaken into tagging these 'objects' so that they can be identified and reused elsewhere. It is expected that projects will have a three-year life cycle to include revision and evaluation. Originally 140 hours were offered for development, with production starting six months before delivery. Starting this far in advance was a big change for many lecturers who were more used to just-in-time preparation. Given the three-stage cycle, 140 hours were offered in the first year; 70 hours in the second;

and ten hours in the third year. It was found though that 140 hours was too much and this is no longer offered. The advantage of this approach has been that it is the lecturers who decide on the priorities and this allows for better planning and allocation of resources. However, this does demand clear project management to ensure that all the necessary information is at hand and control is maintained over the developments.

Supporting change: educational development units

As well as having the vision and the structures to promote change, together with a dedicated budget, another key feature to enable innovation to become embedded within the university is the need to provide support, including organisational structures that can respond quickly and staff with project management skills (Bates, 1997). The location of this educational development support can be provided either through one central unit, or a combination of units that service the whole university or through devolved support units established in faculties, or a combination of both. It has been recognised that the organisational culture of universities often results in very decentralised institutions, yet the very nature of technological innovation demands a whole institution approach to its implementation. This has the potential to cause tension between the faculties and the central units established to implement the change, if not carefully managed (McMurray, 2001).

Within the universities visited we found a variety of organisational structures supporting educational development, but most involved a central unit or a combination of central and faculty based support, as for example, in Deakin and Melbourne.

David Gosling's (2001) survey of UK educational development units in the UK revealed that they were frequently reorganised in an attempt to find the optimum location for support and this was often the case in Australia. Several of the units visited, for example at QUT and Melbourne were still finding their feet as a result of recent mergers or reorganisations of their constituent parts. The reasons for the changes were often presented as a desire to make such units more service-oriented and supportive of faculty developments. In two cases, at Edith Cowan and Wollongong, service level agreements with faculties were reported to be in place in order to achieve this.

Whatever their location or organisation, the critical success factor is how effectively the units collaborate with faculties. We heard some interesting stories. In some cases, academics in the faculty complained that they found it difficult to work with instructional designers. This was because the designers did not have university teaching experience and they tended to represent a transmission view of learning rather than a constructivist approach. This resulted in the lecturers reporting that they felt marginalised. This tension was more obvious between the central units and Faculties of Education, where members of the faculty could be quite critical of the approach adopted by the central unit, both of the pedagogic approach underlying the promotion of e-learning, and of the way the unit approached staff development.

Supporting change: staff development

In order to promote change at the individual level, appropriate staff development for new teaching methods should be in place (Bates, 1997; Cox et al. 1999). However, changing

academic practice is a complex process, especially at a time when perceptions of academic work are changing (Martin, 1999; Coaldrake and Steadman, 1999; Taylor, 1999). Lecturers are being encouraged to learn to use the technology and develop appropriate pedagogical approaches in the face of uncertainty or scepticism about its value to student learning and its impact on the academic workload. In this context, staff development should concentrate on developing conceptions of learning and learners, and then demonstrate how technology may be used to promote learning. (Taylor, Lopez and Quadrelli, 1996, pxiii). But even if an appropriate staff development programme is in place, lecturers need to see that putting effort into changing their teaching practice is valued and that the effort is rewarded.

As evidence of embedding innovation and change, we considered the nature of the staff development activities provided by the units. We looked at the extent to which they offered skills training in the technology of e-learning, focusing on the e-learning platform and the design of web-based/multimedia resources, compared with the extent to which they offered a wider staff development programme focused on pedagogical principles drawing on evidence of research into learning (Littlejohn and Cameron, 1999). In the latter, we looked at the location of the scholarly or research base from which the development was offered. A tension between these foci was observed. Sometimes restructuring of the units had resulted in a move away from an academic, research base because they were perceived to have lost their emphasis on servicing the corporate agenda.

Whatever form it took, staff development was regarded as essential to the successful implementation of e-learning. At Deakin it was estimated that the cost of implementing the new learning management system over the next 5 years will be AU$10m. The cost of the software licence is an insignificant part of this, as the major expense is in staff development.

Many of the universities offered award bearing courses, Post Graduate certificates in learning and teaching, for staff to undertake. In some cases, for example Edith Cowan, this was compulsory for new staff.

The speed of adoption and sustainability of levels of support is causing problems for some universities. At Edith Cowan the fast uptake of Blackboard is having an enormous impact on the demand for professional development. An effort is going to be made to attract more senior staff for the workshops and focus on aspects of quality and strategy rather than the technological aspects. A dramatic increase in demand for e-learning was also causing concern at Wollongong, where it was estimated that, in terms of real changes in teaching and learning, there will be three cycles before the use of WebCT is fully integrated into the teaching. So far, Wollongong has managed to implement a high percentage of its courses in WebCT in a co-ordinated and supportive way, but it is recognised that maintaining the flexibility of this support for both staff and students may be more difficult as resources become stretched.

Potential issues were also identified at Monash, where after extensive use of WebCT, the desire to introduce greater quality improvements into online education was evident. However, it was recognised that this may result in lecturers feeling that they have less control over their subject content, if not handled sensitively.

The need to focus on audiences with different motivations was also recognised. For example, SCU is now in the phase where they have to

influence the late- and non-adopters so a model with a champion in each faculty is being considered. At Monash, where pilot e-learning projects were being undertaken with the more IT focused faculties, the way forward for encouraging further adoption by other less IT focused faculties was uncertain. Similarly, Murdoch has been using WebCT since 1997 but the uptake is regarded as slow, only increasing from 23 courses in 1997 to 141 in 1999. The reasons for this were given as the need to use HTML input initially. This was fine for 10% of academics who were enthusiasts, but since1999 the Murdoch Online Mainstreaming project was initiated to ensure that there would be help from central resources to engage more of the mainstream body of lecturers.

We also saw some extensive change programmes organised at faculty level, where the enthusiasm of lecturers was the starting point for developments, for example in the Education Faculties at UTS and QUT.

Reward and recognition for teaching

Even if appropriate support and staff development opportunities are in place, lecturers need to see that putting effort into changing their teaching practice is valued and that the effort is rewarded. We identified a number of different mechanisms for achieving this in the universities visited, apart from the funding of lecturers' projects. For example, at QUT, promotion criteria had been reviewed to include scholarship of teaching. Another of the most innovative approaches we heard about, also at QUT, was the annual Compassionate Pioneer award, where staff who had been helpful to others in using ICT for learning were nominated either by their colleagues or by students for a prize. There were also several examples of

Fellowships awarded for learning and teaching innovation. At a national level, several universities were proudly displaying evidence of winning national awards. One distinctive approach to rewarding lecturers was taken at Melbourne, where the university was very rigorous in identifying the intellectual property implications of the multimedia resources produced and offered lecturers a proportion of the income generated if the product was a commercial success outside the university.

Links between educational development and other support services

The final strategic consideration is the need for the e-learning support initiative for staff to be linked to e-learning support provision for students, to ensure that the students have sufficient skills and knowledge to be able to take advantage of the more flexible and independent learning opportunities offered. We observed some interesting examples of where this was happening. Sometimes it involved a change of roles, so at Melbourne, the subject librarians had taken on a new role to support lecturers in identifying online resources. At QUT, the recent alignment of Library, IT and educational development services was being cemented through a month-long job rotation of the senior managers of those services, so they came to have a first hand understanding of each other's strengths and issues. In many instances, information and IT skills were core elements of the curriculum.

Conclusion

The strategic implementation of e-learning is being addressed in Australian universities in much the same way as in the UK and the Netherlands. The same factors of senior management support and the availability of resources are key elements of success, as is the appropriate mix of central and devolved support for innovation. However, the most critical factor is winning the hearts and minds of lecturers, who not only have to adapt their teaching methods, but also, in many cases, have to revise their long held conceptions of what teaching is. This culture change is the most difficult, and as in the UK and Netherlands, you could find universities where it was apparently happening, and some, where it was clearly remaining a challenge.

The very difficult nature of this challenge was illustrated for me by an episode I observed during the weekend break in the middle of our tour. I was walking on the beach at Noosa and stopped briefly to watch a surfing instructor giving a lesson. The two women students had their surfboards flat on the sand and were trying to balance on them. The instructor said, encouragingly, 'It's not much different to being on the water really, its sort of all in your head'. I wondered what strategies he was going to use to ensure that the necessary skills and knowledge were transferred from his head to theirs, and I hope he succeeded, because they did not look too safe, even on dry land. Similarly, it is easy for senior university managers to write their vision statements about e-learning, but unless staff and students are enabled to develop the skills, knowledge and motivation to engage with it, it will remain a vision rather than a reality.

References

Bates, A.W., 1997. Restructuring the university for technological change. Paper presented to the Carnegie Foundation for the Advancement of Teaching, 18-20 June, London. Available at: **http://bates.cstudies.ubc.ca/**

Bottomley, J., Spratt, T, C., Rice, M., 1999. Strategies for effecting strategic change in teaching practices: Case studies at Deakin University. Interactive Learning Environments, 7 (2-3) 227-247.

Coaldrake, P. and Steadman, L., 1999. Academic work in the Twenty-first Century: Changing roles and policies. Canberra: Higher Education Division, Department of Education, Training and Youth Affairs. **www.dest.gov.au/archive/highered/occpaper/99H/academic.pdf.** Last accessed 28th January 2002

Collis, B., Peters, O., and Pals, N., 2000. Influences on the educational use of the WWW, Email and videoconferencing. Innovations in Education and Teaching International, 37 (2) 108-119.

Cox, M., Preston, C. and Cox, K., 1999. What motivates teachers to use ICT? British Educational Research Association Annual Conference, University of Sussex at Brighton, September 2-5 1999.

Littlejohn, A. and Cameron, S., 1999. Supporting strategic change and cultural change: the Strathclyde learning technology initiative as a model. Association for Learning Technology Journal, 7 (3) 64-74.

Gosling, D., 2001. Educational development units in the UK – what are they doing five years on? International Journal for Academic Development, 6(1), 74-90.

McMurray, D.W., 2001. The importance of 'goodness of fit' between organisational culture and climate in the management of change: a case study in the development of online learning. Association for Learning Technology Journal, 9 (1), 73-83.

Martin, E., 1999. Changing academic work: developing the learning university. Buckingham: SRHE & Open University Press

Moore, G.A., 1991. Crossing the chasm. New York: Harper Business.

Taylor, P. G., Lopez, L. and Quadrelli, C., 1996. Flexibility, technology and academics' perspectives: Tantalising tales and muddy maps. Canberra: Higher Education Division, Evaluation and Investigation Program, Department of Employment, Education and Youth Affairs,: Australian Government Publishing Service.

Taylor, P., 1999. Making sense of academic life: academics, universities and change. Buckingham: SRHE & Open University Press

Watson, D., 2000. Managing strategy. Buckingham: Open University Press.

3. Partnerships in the Australian Tertiary-Education Sector

Betty Collis and Robert Harding

Abstract

What motivates different forms of partnerships in the Australian tertiary-education sector? What are key types of partnerships? How important is technology to support the work of the partnerships? This perspective report begins by noting some of the key motivations for partnerships before focusing on two key categories of partnerships for the Australian tertiary-education sector: (a) among educational institutions, particularly between an Australian institution and institutions outside of Australia, and (b) industry partnerships. Different initiatives for stimulating and supporting partnerships are noted, both at the sector level as well as in institutions themselves. The role of communication and information technologies in the partnerships is an on-going point of attention. Technology, particularly web-based resources and systems, are indispensable for the partnerships.

The context for partnerships in the Australian tertiary sector

Tertiary-education institutions are separate entities, each concerned about its own profile and viability. What motivates these institutions in Australia to seek partnerships either with other educational institutions or training centres or with other partners such as public agencies or the corporate sector? Three major types of motivations were identified. For each of these, technology plays a role.

Government policy and funding

Unquestionably, the most important single driver for partnerships in the Australian tertiary-education system is the Federal Government's funding policy. This funding policy requires the higher-education sector to handle more students and improve 'quality' while keeping funding the same or at reduced levels, and also expects individuals to contribute more personally to the cost of their higher and further education. 'The balance of university funding has shifted such that public investment in teaching has reduced while funding for university research and fee-based teaching has increased. It is important for universities to have a range of income sources... Income from fee-paying students is an important and growing source of university revenue. Overseas fee-paying students contribute 79% of the fee-paying revenue' (Australian Vice-Chancellors' Committee, 2002a).

For research, the picture is more complicated, as a substantial amount of money comes from Commonwealth (central government) funding with the requirement that private sector partners be involved as paying partners. 'The increasing proportion of research funding from other sources reflects universities' increasing involvement with industry...Over the past decade, Australia's universities have become more involved with the private sector and the community. They are now balancing the more traditional forms of basic research with contract work, consultations, and research project involving specific commercial objectives' (Australian Vice-Chancellors' Committee, 2002b).

Thus Australian universities need external funding sources to meet their budgets.

Internationalisation

The need for fee-paying students relates directly to another major aspect of the context for Australian tertiary education: Internationalisation. Most fee-paying students are from outside Australia; in the decade between 1990 and 2000 the number of international fee-paying students rose from 25,000 to 95,000. In some institutions this is 25% of the student population (James, 2002). This relates to the strategic importance of internationalisation to the university sector. 'Universities have a heavy responsibility in relation to internationalisation for not only are they at the forefront of one of Australia's fastest growing export 'industries', the export of education services, but also they must prepare young Australians to be able to operate effectively internationally as well as to maintain research and technology capabilities of highest world standards' (Australian Vice-Chancellors' Committee, 2000a). The top two outcomes of the Australian Vice-Chancellors Committee (AVCC) for International Relations 2000-2002 Strategic Plan are:

1. Strong higher education sector strategic partnerships between the AVCC and counterparts overseas, recognising Australia's commitment to the Asia-Pacific and Indian Ocean regions.

2. Strong links between universities in Australia and overseas.

Thus the strategic policy of universities strongly motivates partnerships of various sorts.

Industry-tertiary sector relationships

A final aspect of the Australian context that is important for analysing partnerships is the general relation between the tertiary-education sector and industry. In Australia, 'Vocational education and training is 'education and training for work'. It exists to develop and recognise the competencies or skills of learners. It has traditionally been seen as post-secondary, non-university education and training, focusing on apprenticeships. But reforms in the past decade now see vocational education and training programs offered in secondary schools, stronger

links with university study options and six levels of qualifications offered in most industries, including high growth, new economy industries' (Australian National Training Authority (ANTA), 2002; www.anta.gov.au/). While universities had traditionally seen themselves as having a 'hands-off' attitude to workplace-related education, leaving this to the Technical and Further Education (TAFE) sector, the ANTA website makes clear that universities are now beginning to recognise the strategic importance of involvement with workplace-oriented training and professional development.

Thus the context for higher education in Australia makes partnerships not only highly stimulated but also necessary for the sector. These can be seen in different forms: international education consortia which may or may not involve commercialisation, corporate universities where a major player is a multinational company, university networks of various sorts, and start-up ventures with technology companies (Cunningham, et al., 2000). Crock, Joughin, Edwards, and Curtis (2001) conclude that 'the obvious and immediate benefit of forming partnerships is the economic sustainability of higher education institutions' (p. 93). 'Universities themselves are increasingly collaborating, networking and partnering. These activities are becoming interdependent and some lines of demarcation are blurring both among different universities and between universities and other institutions' (Galagher, 2000, p. 42).

Technology and partnerships

Technology has many functions in the support of partnerships in Australian higher education. Five particular sets of functions are shown in Figure 7.

The first type of technology use is exclusively via websites. All of the Australian higher-education

1. Information dissemination and communication with the public

2. Learning-support: Course-support systems and tools, Learning-specific resources

3. Tools and resources for partnership support: Web environments, groupware, communication systems

4. Systems for management and support services (portals, registration, library access)

5. Technology as a focus of the partnership

Figure 7. Technology support for partnerships in Australian higher education

institutions make sophisticated use of web technology to advertise their services and provide easy methods for contacts from the public (see www.avcc.edu.au/australias_unis/individual_unis/ for links to the homesites of all the universities). The homesites are of a high standard, offer an extensive amount of information, and frequently make use of multimedia resources. One of the common features of all the homesites is information about the partnerships in which the university is involved. The homesites play an important public-relations and advertising role. With regard to the second type of technology use, the Australian institutions are in different levels of centralisation with respect to the use of web-based course-management systems, but all universities use web technology in some way to support off-shore learning partnerships. Sometimes the learning is extensively accessed via the Australian university's web-based course-management system; other times web tools and resources are used for different aspects of learning support such as facilitating communication with Australian instructors. Again, web technology is a key tool for making education partnerships possible when the students involved are at different locations. The third type of technology use is focused on the needs of the partners themselves, for their own internal purposes. Regular use is made of different sorts of communication tools, web

environments, and groupware tools to support partner activities, even when the partners are in the same region. The fourth type of technology use relates to the increasingly sophisticated systems being used to coordinate educational services. Sometimes these tools relate more to the needs of the organisation such as the system developed at Charles Sturt University to keep track of student registration and fee payments in a wide range of different course offerings. Other times the technology functions as a portal to provide access to a wide range of support services to students wherever their location. Remote access to library resources is common, as is access to student records and tools for remote registration in courses. Every university has systems of these sorts in differing combinations of functionalities. Finally, technology can also be a focus of a partnership itself, such as when institutions work together on the development, procurement and or maintenance of jointly used technology-based learning resources. An example of this is the partnership between the University of Melbourne and Monash University, where a collaboration between the medical faculties has led to the common development of a large number of electronic learning resources (mostly not yet web based).

In this section we have given an overview of the context for partnerships in the Australian tertiary-education sector and of major ways in which technology facilitates those partnerships. In the next section we look at specific examples.

Key types of partnerships

We focus on partnerships for Australian tertiary educational institutions in two major categories: with other educational institutions, for course delivery; and with industry and the corporate sector, for both courses and research.

Partnerships among educational institutions

Partnerships among educational institutions can involve groupings of Australian partners or partnerships that also include partners from outside of Australia.

Within Australia: Australian educational institutions are partnering with each other in a number of ways. Galagher (2000, p. 42) notes that in some local areas (Perth, Brisbane and Adelaide), there is a certain amount of sharing of administrative and technology-supported services (for common purchasing, publishing, cleaning, fleet management, and financial and human resources services). This is an example of Type 5 of the categories of technology in partnerships (Figure 7). Networking among Australian universities is occurring for marketing, benchmarking, lobbying, and strategy formation. Galagher cites the formation of the Group of Eight universities (www.go8.edu.au/), the Australian Technology Network of universities, and the Group of Regional Universities as major examples. In these partnerships, strategic use is made of partnership Websites for external profiling and communication (Type 1, Figure 7). Often there are closed areas of such Websites to facilitate the partners themselves, for example for

access to partnership resources and to support partnership work (Type 3, Figure 7). Universities may also partner around a technology focus, such as the Melbourne-Monash partnership for medical-school learning resources, or the joint project between Edith Cowan University and Wollongong University, to study the role of information and communication technologies in flexible learning (Type 5, Figure 7).

Formal links with universities outside of Australia: Every Australian university has established partnerships with other universities outside of Australia (AVCC, 2001a). As of May 2001, Australian universities had 3895 formal agreements with overseas higher-education institutions. Figure 8 shows the growth of these formal partnerships over the last two decades.

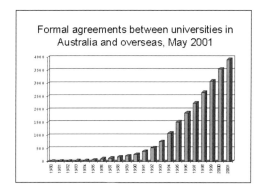

Figure 8. Formal partnerships between Australian and external universities. Source: AVCC, 2001a

Although Asian partners are important to Australian universities, The USA is the most favoured source of university partnerships (see Figure 9).

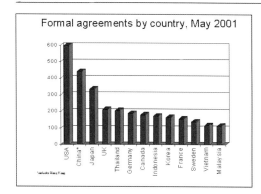

Formal agreements by country, May 2001

Figure 9. Partnerships between Australian and external universities. Source: AVCC, 2001a

In these partnerships, the particular emphasis has been placed on the benefit of student and staff exchange and research collaboration. Staff exchange is the major category. Technology use is primarily of Type 3, Figure 7.

While intellectual cross-fertilisation occurs, there does not seem to be a particular financial benefit to the Australian institutions from these partnerships. In contrast is a third major type of partnership among educational institutions: the offshore course-delivery programmes.

Offshore programs: As of May 2001 Australian universities had 1,009 offshore programs with overseas higher-education institutions (AVCC, 2001b). Offshore programs are generally of two major types: (a) Affiliated college or third-party franchises, or (b) one-on-one model (source: K. Dillon, Charles Sturt University (CSU)). Dillon describes a typical situation at CSU with regard to the first type:

'For the affiliated college model, we work with an overseas institution that wants to offer some of our courses or programmes to its own students...The model involves CSU providing the learning materials (print and online), the teaching expertise, and standardised assessment. There is a 'subject convener' from CSU who has the responsibility for liaison with subject coordinators and teaching staff at both institutions, to coordinate subject development, including assignments and examinations, so that the CSU degree can be awarded...CSU staff go to the partner institution and sometimes do some of the teaching'.

The second model of international partnerships with regard to offshore courses is the one-to-one model, in which the Australian university supplies everything, and the off shore group is treated as distance education students or as on campus students of a local branch of the home Australian university. As an example, at CSU there is a major partnership with the School of Professional and Continuing Education in Hong Kong of the first of these variations, for both IT programmes and library science. An example of the second variation is that of Monash University Malaysia. Monash University Malaysia was established on February 23, 1998 in Bandar Sunway upon invitation of the Malaysian Government. Its establishment is a joint venture between Monash University in Australia and the Sunway Group. As one of the eight Monash campuses, Monash Malaysia is subject to the university for all matters related to academic development, teaching and support. In its website, (www.monash.edu.my/) it describes its program as:

'Monash University Malaysia offers its students the exciting opportunity to study overseas as part of the Monash degree. An international experience while you are a student is a great way to broaden your outlook and enrich your life. There are two types of programs:

131

A. Intercampus Exchange

Monash students studying at the Malaysian campus may be able to undertake part of their studies at a Monash University campus in Australia. Subject to faculty requirements and after completing the first year of study, students may spend up to two semesters in Australia.

B. Study Abroad Program

Monash currently has exchange partnerships with over 80 universities in Asia, Europe, the Middle East and North America, as well as a range of fee-paying study abroad options for undergraduate students. Exchanges offer students the opportunity to study for one semester or a full year.

Students who wish to participate in the program must be enrolled students of Monash University Malaysia and have paid all fees before leaving for overseas university destinations. Participants of the Intercampus Exchange Program (part (a) above) do not pay overseas tuition fees; students are not transferring their enrolment, they remain as Monash Malaysia students, but will spend one or two semesters studying at another Monash campus'.

The 'latest news' offered on the partnership website is: 'Interview sessions in India & Sri Lanka' and 'Interview sessions and career talks in Indonesia', indicating the regional orientation of the campus. Monash Malaysia is expecting enrolments to grow from the current 1700 to 2500 within three years, and there are plans with local backers to have land available for a campus for up to 8000 students.

Individual faculties within a university can also have their own educational partnerships and offshore programs. An example is the Deakin University Faculty of Business and Law that provides a page of links to its partnership institutions on its Website

(www.deakin.edu.au/bus_law/partners.htm) and describes itself as having 'developed strong partnerships with leading universities, Technical and Further Education (TAFE) colleges, businesses, professional societies, and private educational providers, both on-shore and off-shore.' Among its 'partnerships in international education' it cites arrangements with Disted-Stamford College, Penang, Malaysia (since 1987); Technology Management Centre, Singapore; and CPA Australia and Capital University, Beijing. All of these involve joint initiatives with an offshore partner, resulting in a Deakin University degree.

For these course-related partnerships, Technology Types 1, 2, and 4 from Figure 7 are all important. Type 1 technology use is increasingly critical as a marketing tool, while Types 2 and 4 are needed to offer services and support to off campus students. Charles Sturt University is a strong example as is the University of Southern Queensland, Monash University, and Deakin Universities.

There has been consistent growth in the number of new offshore programs since 1992. They are a significant source of fee-paying student income for Australian universities. More than 70% of all offshore programs of Australian universities are in Singapore, Malaysia and Hong Kong. A recent example is RMIT International University Vietnam (www.mpu.rmit.edu.au/index.html). RMIT is ready to begin construction of the new AUS$31.5 million campus, which is scheduled to open in September 2003. Figure 10 shows the distribution by country in May 2001. A total of 37 Australian universities are involved in the current offshore programs (a spreadsheet with names of all Australian-overseas partnerships for offshore programs is available at the AVCC website, www.avcc.edu.au/policies_activities/international_relations/internationalisation_initiatives/offshor.htm).

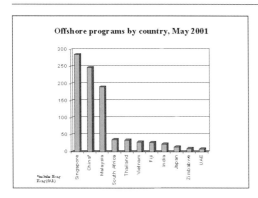

Offshore programs by country, May 2001

Figure 10. Offshore education programs, Australian universities Source: AVCC, 2001b

Although most of the partnerships between universities in general or for offshore degree programs are the initiatives of the individual universities, in some cases there is also a central framework via the AVCC (Australian Vice-Chancellors' Committee, the council of Australia's university presidents). As an example, in 2000 a collaborative framework for partnerships with Indonesian universities was extended:

"Since the late 1980s, the Indonesia/Australia education relationship has broadened. While Australian Government scholarships for Indonesian students remain an important feature, there has been sharp growth in the number of Indonesian university students independently choosing to study in Australia. Numbers have grown from 2,991 in 1994 to 8,088 in 1999, generating an estimated AU$160 million in foreign earnings for Australia last year. Over the same period the number of formal links between universities in Australia and Indonesia has grown exponentially, from 52 to 178. These links embrace staff and student exchange as well as research collaboration" (AVCC, 2000b).

Other partnerships relating to educational delivery: In addition to partnerships for offshore degree programs, there are a number of other partnerships involving Australian universities and other universities and focused on increasing the range of Australia's educational programs. Technology use in Types 1, 2, and 4 of Figure 7 is critical to the functioning of the partnerships. Two examples are Universitas 21 and Australian National Universities (ANU) initiative as part of the World Bank's Virtual Colombo Plan.

Universitas 21: The website of this international partnership (www.universitas.edu.au/) describes Universitas 21 as:

"an international network of leading research-intensive universities. Incorporated in Guernsey, it has 18 member universities in 10 countries. The Company's core business is provision of a pre-eminent brand for educational services supported by a strong quality assurance framework…This network allows member universities to pursue significant global initiatives that would be beyond their individual capabilities. Universitas 21 is now positioned to take a leading role in the emerging global market for educational services because of the high level of common interest between its members, and because they share a vision of the future of higher education and the role of established campus-based universities in it."

Three Australian universities are involved in Universitas 21: University of Melbourne, University of New South Wales, and University of Queensland. The University of Melbourne has chosen to invest all of its international educational partnerships within the Universitas context. However, the Universitas 21 initiative has generated some concern within Australia. Students at the University of Queensland demonstrated during a university board meeting that 'being part of this consortium will only jeopardise the reputation of member universities... According to the NUS (National Union of Students), Universitas 21 is just one more step initiated by university administrators and 'profit-driven companies' to further deregulate the international education system' (Sydney Morning Herald, 28/02/2001, www.smh.com.au)

Virtual Colombo Plan: As another example of an extended partnership, the Australian National University (ANU) is setting up a collaborative program under the auspices of the World Bank's Virtual Colombo Plan for Internet-delivered education for developing countries, launched in Sydney in 2001. The Website for the ANU initiative (http://news.com.au/common/printpage/0,6093,3806897,00.html) describes the partnership as follows:

> "A potentially trend-setting way for Australian universities to reach offshore students is in the offing - live lectures via satellite to roomfuls of students, with simultaneous teaching contributions or discussion possible at several sites. The Australian National University – the local hub for the program – is trying to interest other universities, which have been cautious, in providing content. ANU held a meeting with about 50 university and World Bank representatives in Canberra in January 2002. Universities indicating interest so far are Canberra, Charles Sturt, Curtin, Deakin, Edith Cowan, Monash, RMIT and Southern Queensland. Universities' offshore campuses could become hubs. Education promoter IDP Australia is also holding discussions with ANU. The program enables video-conference links with specially equipped offshore lecture theatres. Australia has committed AU$200 million to the plan. The network, supporters

say, will let Australian universities and organisations deliver programs to audiences now hard to reach. So far there are about 30 distance learning centres, including the ANU, with a target of 150. AusAid may fund two in Papua New Guinea and ANU wants it to help fund work in East Timor, which is also getting a centre. The centres consist of rooms for video-conferencing and Internet-linked personal computers. Teaching by video-conference will be backed by Internet-based tutoring, sometimes using in-country teachers."

The success of the ANU initiative is not yet known. However, the World Bank initiative to which it relates (The Global Development Learning Network, www.gdln.org/locations.html) is thriving internationally in 36 countries and focuses on partnerships between Western universities and developing countries for Internet-supported learning. Thus the ANU initiative is in a solid context. In contrast, although started in 1997, the Universitas 21 initiative, at least according to its website, still seems to be at the 'forming agreements' stage. Staff and student exchanges seem to be occurring, while other activities appear to be still at the preparatory level.

Clearly, the Universitas 21 and ANU partnership as part of the Virtual Colombo Plan can only exist via the use of technology to support participation in distributed learning situations (Type 2, Figure 7); to support common management and service functions (Type 4, Figure 7); and to attract clients and attention to the partnerships (Type 1, Figure 7).

A commercial academic partnership: In possible the first Australian example of this type of partnership, Curtin University of Technology has signed a contract to deliver training worldwide for a multinational company. The Master of Technology (Petroleum Technology) will be awarded to those Shell engineers who are undergoing a four-year in-house course which covers key areas of expertise necessary for the petroleum industry. The eight-unit degree consists of a maximum of five Shell units and three Curtin units. Some units will be taught by Shell and examined by Curtin academics, while other units will be taught by the University in various locations around the world. The degree will run from Curtin's new Sarawak campus. (See http://newsbytes.curtin.edu.au/archive/shell.htm)

Other partnerships relating to educational support: Charles Sturt University (CSU) provides an interesting example of another kind of community partnership through the Higher School Certificate Project (HSC http://hsc.csu.edu.au/study/). This Project was started by a CSU Pro Vice-Chancellor: who realised that CSU had a role to play in secondary education. This is in the context of CSU's tradition to serve the economically oriented educational needs of its region. The project is a joint institutional project run mainly by DET (The State of NSW's Dept of Education and Training). The HSC site provides resources for rural and regional schools and communities.

Partnerships between the tertiary-education sector and industry: In general, partnerships between the tertiary sector and industry relate to course provision, to research initiatives, or to other forms of collaboration. The TAFE sector is primarily involved in the course-provision partnerships and the university sector in research-oriented partnerships.

Partnerships between the TAFE sector and industry for course provision: There are many examples of partnerships between the TAFE sector and industry for course provision. As an example, the Gordon Institute of TAFE (www.gordontafe.edu.au/index.cfm) in Geelong, Victoria, has an extensive relationship with the Learning and Development unit of the Shell Refining (Australia) Pty Ltd at Geelong in Victoria. The partnership involves more than course provision, as it is primarily focused on a consulting relationship with regard to the overall instructional approaches of the Shell Learning and Development unit. Another example is the TAFE Southern Australia (www.tafe.sa.gov.au/customisedservices/) which 'offers specialised training for industry, businesses and government departments, providing customised services and consulting services to meet a diverse range of training needs'. Many TAFEs develop their programs in direct partnership with an industry branch. For example, the Training Design Department at Wodonga Institute of TAFE in Victoria was awarded a first place prize at the 2001 'Automotive Training Australia Innovation In Training Awards' ceremony for their 'Fault Diagnostic Resource Package' (www. wodonga.tafe.edu.au/news/20024319334.htm). A range of partnership models between TAFEs and industry in the South Australia area can be seen at the Web site www.wfworldcongress.com/tours-sthaus.htm. The TAFE-partnership-industry links include, beyond the individual TAFEs, also many international partnerships such as the Indonesia Australia Partnership for Skills Development Program (www.ita.edu.au/project/iapsd.htm).

As the majority of these partnerships involve on-site training within the companies involved, the use of technology is generally limited to occasional use of products on CD-ROMs or simulation software specially made for the sector or company involved (Technology Type 2, Figure 7). There appears to be less use of web technology in partnerships between the TAFE and industry than is the case with the support of off shore programmes for the universities. Internet access in company training settings is not yet common and many of the specially made electronic learning resources make extensive use of video and audio, not felt to be feasible for the level of network access generally available to the clients involved. However, Type 1 (use of the web for information and communication with the public) is well established. A search via Google of TAFE and AUSTRALIA and INDUSTRY and PARTNERSHIPS brings up over 9,000 links.

A number of universities, such as Deakin, work closely with TAFEs. Deakin for example has licensed a number of individual TAFE institutes to teach core units in its bachelors' programs. Students are able to transfer to the BCom with full credit upon meeting criteria for successful completion.

Universities and industry partnerships for course delivery: Universities also work directly with industry or government for educational partnerships. As an example, at Charles Sturt University, the 'Police Academy' is run entirely by CSU under contract to the NSW police force. This partnership also involves the funding of a chair at CSU. Also, the extensive program at CSU relating to the wine industry is 50% funded by the industry itself. Environment studies are partly funded by a partnership with the NSW Department of Agriculture. At Deakin, tailored

Masters programs for industry partners such as Coca Cola and the Australian Insurance Institute (www.deakin.edu.au/bus_law/partners.htm) are examples. Also at Deakin, the Coles Institute was established in 1999 as a partnership organisation, between Deakin and Coles' supermarket division to provide a full range of certificate, diploma and degree courses for over 52,000 supermarket staff. At the University of Melbourne, the Institute of Land and Food Resources (a partnership between Victorian College of Agriculture and Horticulture and the university's departments of Agriculture and Forestry) has eight campuses in rural and metropolitan Victoria, more than 400 staff, 1,300 undergraduate and postgraduate students and 10,000 students in vocational courses.

In these situations, technology is used for communication and public information (Type 1, Figure 7) and in various ways for some learning support (Type 2, Figure 7), generally similar to the types of technology use seen in TAFE-industry training partnerships.

Partnerships with industry for research: Partnerships with industry are important for the research activities of universities as well as for income from course provision. Approximately 90% of research in Australian universities is carried out via PhD students, and of these maybe 10% are funded by industry, but this varies by institution and sector. Research-oriented industry partnerships can occur in many forms. Some examples are:

At Charles Sturt University, the Cooperative Research Centre for Sustainable Rice Production. Member organisations include CSU, The University of Sydney, the CSIRO Division of Plant Industry, CSIRO Land and Water, NSW Agriculture, the NSW Department of Land and

Water Conservation, Rural Industries Research and Development Corporation and the Ricegrowers' Cooperative Limited. This seven-year research partnership provides enough money to support 15 Masters students and 15 PhD students.

At Queensland University of Technology, 30-40% of its research is funded externally, much of this via government 'linkage grants' that require partnerships with industry and matching funds.

At Griffiths University, a large project funded by AstraZeneca, a Swedish pharmaceutical company provides research funding for biomedical investigations (www.az.gu.edu.au). This is a major partnership: AstraZeneca has funded one five-year cycle beginning in 1993 and also a second cycle from 1998-2003. The contribution is $AU8.5 million per year.

For these partnerships, there is usually a public website for the profiling of the partnership (Type 1, Figure 7). Beyond this, partners make use of various technologies to support their own collaborative activities (Type 3, Figure 7).

Other sorts of industry partnerships: There are many other examples of partnerships involving a blend of education, research, and community/sector service, supported in various ways by technology. Some examples include:

At the Queensland University of Technology, the 'creative industries' program (www.creativeindustries.qut.com/) involves different layers of government (state, Brisbane) and other partners with the university, developing a new Faculty of Creative Industries as part of the initiative.(www.creativeindustries. qut.com/partnerships/).

The Australian Technology Park, Sydney (www.atp.com.au/) is a collaborative venture of three Sydney universities (UNSW, UTS, UofSydney), some TAFEs, and government. Its purpose is to provide an incubator environment for spin-offs from university research, often in partnership with a company. For example, the Phonetics Research Centre located at the Park has funding from Telstra and Opta (telecom companies). This is an example of technology as a focus of the partnership (Technology Type 5, Figure 7).

At Griffiths University, the Logan Campus has attracted various sorts of external funding including from Sun Microsystems who donated AU$220,000 to have its name attached to a major computer-work room. (Technology Type 5, Figure 7). A new graduate certificate relating to case-study expertise for enterprises is being funded by external sources as well (Taylor & Blaik, 2002).

At the University of Melbourne, pharmaceutical companies make substantial donations to its medical schools and their research. The Bio21 Precinct Project (www.unimelb.edu.au/ ExtRels/Media/00media/00june26b.html) is described on its website as 'Australia's largest and most sophisticated biomedical research and biotechnological development'. It is funded in part by leading biotechnology industry interests, AU$262 million. The Bio21 Project will link interdisciplinary basic science in the university's new Bio21 Molecular Science and Biotechnology Institute with work in a range of major medical research institutes and in the Royal Melbourne and other major hospitals.

There are 50-60 'collaborative research centres' around the country, funded by a collection of monies, from government, companies, and 'in kind' contributions of the universities. Many of these are funded by the Commonwealth Scientific Industrial Research Organisation (CSIRO); (see the next section). Money is mainly used to fund PhD research. Technology provides the normal support for academic work, where communication and web access is essential for normal functioning.

Initiatives for stimulating and supporting partnerships

Because of the importance of partnerships, particularly with industry, to the tertiary sector in Australia, there are many different forms of stimulation and support available. Some is central, to the entire sector, while other examples can be found within individual universities. A particular example within universities is the development of a corporate arm to stimulate and facilitate entrepreneurial commercial partnerships involving the university.

Support and stimulation at the sector level
There are a number of initiatives and agencies involved in the stimulation and support of partnerships. From the stimulation side, major examples are the national research funding bodies that explicitly call for industry contributions and partnerships in many of the funding opportunities. A major example here is the Australian Research Council's (www.arc.gov.au/) Strategic Partnerships with Industry – Research and Training (SPIRT) (www.ofs.mq/edu.au/ofs_web/GrantManagement/gm_stratgic_partnerships_with_indu.htm) scheme that encourages co-operative research alliances between universities and industry organisations. For collaborative research, the Industry Partner contribution must match the amount sought from the Commonwealth on a dollar-for-dollar basis. Similar conditions apply for Linkage Grants (www.arc.gov.au/ncgp/outcomes/feed_lp.htm) which also fund collaborative projects between university researchers and industry partners. The linkage grants website lists the success rate per university for the awards announced in April 2002 (overall success rate was approximately 50%). The universities with the highest success rates in April 2002 were ANU-IAS, University of Melbourne, Macquarie, University of Newcastle, UNSW, and Central Queensland University. Industry partner commitment is worth 25% of the scoring for the awards.

Technology is a management tool (Type 4, Figure 7) and a public-communication tool (Type 1 Figure 7) for these funding agencies.

In addition to stimulating partnerships via funding mechanisms, the Australian government provides support for partnership initiatives, particularly those in which an Australian institution wishes to increase its presence in offshore or other forms of international education. This occurs via the agency called Australian Education International (http://aei.dest.gov.au/general/about/AboutAEI.htm).

Support for industry training relationships is provided by several agencies. The major one is the Australian National Training Authority (ANTA, www.anta.gov.au/) whose website is a portal to a wide variety of services. Also of support to training partnerships is the National Centre for Vocational Education Research (NCVER, www.ncver.edu.au/) whose Website includes links to the reports from funded research projects involving universities or other 'suitably qualified and experienced researchers' as well as opportunities to compete for new rounds of funding. The NCVER also supports a national conference on training research and makes the proceedings available via the website (www.ncver.edu.au/news/conf/index.htm).

Support to the entire Australian education sector is available via education.au.limited (www.educationau.edu.au/business.html) 'a company owned by the Australian education and training Ministers. In particular, the company was set up to foster collaboration and cooperation in the use of the Internet in education and training and to implement joint activities, products and services of the network of education and training authorities known as EdNA (Education Network Australia).' The EdNa portal (www.edna.edu.au/) contains extensive resources and information, much of which can be supportive to partnership activities.

Open Learning Australia (OLA) is an example of a support service that is itself a partnership among universities, it is a company owned by seven Australian universities: Curtin University of Technology, Griffith University, Macquarie University, Monash University, RMIT University, Swinburne University of Technology; and the University of South Australia. OLA operates in the fee-paying sector of the higher education market. OLA works with over 32 Australian universities and providers of vocational education to give learners access to a range of off campus studies that can be credited towards formal qualifications. OLA markets courses, enrols students and collects fees while the academic institutions provide study materials and tuition. 'OLA is in the process of implementing a system that provides potential and existing students with an online interface to the services offered by the Company and allows registered students to gain online access to courses, personal information and academic progress. The system known as the OLA Learning Portal will become progressively available through 2002. The system is conceived as fully conforming to the Shareable Content Object Reference Model initiative (SCORM)

promoted by the US Department of Defence and the companion IMS Metadata Standards' (Beck, Baker, Radford, & Costigan, 2002).

In these examples of sector-wide support services, the use of technology to provide portal-type access to a wide range of services and resources relates to Technology (Type 4, Figure 7). Frequently the service only exists in terms of its interface with its clients via the web-based portal.

Support and stimulation within the institutions

Within tertiary-education institutions themselves there are many different support structures to stimulate and provide services for industry partnerships. At Charles Sturt University, the Farrier Centre (http://farrier.csu.edu.au/), a research centre for agriculture, illustrates one model. The Centre itself is funded by the university, but serves as a unit to bring in projects and funding from industry and government partners. Another model relates to providing different service units. The University of Melbourne illustrates this, with at least the following units directly relating to partnership aspects:

Commercialisation support including ownership issues www.unimelb.edu.au/research/uni.only /ridg/eo

Negotiation of intellectual property agreements (based on a thorough legal document) for collaborative developments with strategic partners including Monash University and Universitas 21 members.

MEI Ltd: Commercialisation services including the identification and incubation of business opportunities and negotiation of commercial agreements. There is also Uniseed Pty Ltd, a joint venture between MEI and UniQuest Ltd of the University of Queensland for funding for 'early stage technology...promising technologies and ideas that have the potential to be the foundation for successful high growth businesses. (www.mei.unimelb.edu.a/)

These services relate to technology as the focus of partnerships (Type 5, Figure 7) and also on issues relating to the ownership of content for Technology (Type 2, Figure 7), where the basic idea of partnerships for joint educational offerings brings with it issues relating to the ownership of intellectual property.

As another example, the University of Southern Australia maintains a number of services for parties wishing to 'do business with UniSA' (www.unisa.edu.au/orc/rbd/Business.htm). On another of its websites (www.unisa.edu.au/orc/iso9001/business.htm), it is stated that 'Give your organisation a leading edge. web technology (Type 1, Figure 7) is essential for contact with the potential clients.

The services offered by the University of Southern Australia for its potential (non-student) customers are formalised in a number of Australian universities via constructions called 'commercial arms'.

Commercial arms

Often partnerships with industry for course delivery are carried out via a commercial arm of the university. A senior administrator of the Australian Catholic University (ACU) noted that 'most Australian universities have a commercial arm, to bring in cash'. At ACU it is called ACUCOM (ACU Commercial). The administrator indicated that external funds and partnerships are "absolutely necessary" for Australian universities. A major example of a commercial arm is Melbourne University Private (MUP, www.muprivate.edu.au/), set up as a 'separate

university', but with a complicated relationship with the University of Melbourne. Its target is corporate clients, 'attempting to provide top-drawer corporate executive education, trading off the prestige of the parent university' (Cunningham, et. al, p. 73). Technology use in these cases works as within any commercial service agency, for public contact and profiling (Type 1, Figure 7) and for maintaining its own processes (Type 3, Figure 7).

MUP is, however, proving controversial. The Education Minister herself has stated that a solely client-driven research agenda is incompatible with the use of the word 'university' in the title. (See www.unimelb.edu.au/vc/2002deansandheadsconference/MUPLInterimReport2002.ppt).

On the other hand the activities that MUP engages in appear to be little different in kind from the commercial activities that many universities engage in. A speculative interpretation is that MUP is an evolutionary experiment in organisational structure for the process of adjusting to new conditions.

Stimulation of research relating to educational uses of technology

Australia has an international reputation for research into learning technologies. Such work does not appear to be the direct driver for the increased use of these technologies though it significantly contributes to their successful use and in some cases will have led implementation. For example, at Edith Cowan (Perth) Prof. Ron Oliver heads the Centre for Research in Information Technology and Communications. A similar situation is in place at Murdoch (Perth) where Dr. Rob Phillips leads the Teaching and Learning Centre. In both these cases these units play a leading role in the implementation of their university's strategy in partnership with support from central administration. The units flourish in structures that take campus-wide use of new technologies seriously and encourage a high profile. In some other cases the technology is seen more as a means and reflective research on how it is used has a low profile.

The partnership aspect here then is between researchers and 'early adopters' on the one hand and central business policy makers on the other. A successful partnership naturally benefits both partners and their university's operation. The international community is also a partner here in some sense through the normal means of academic publication and exchange.

Implications

The study trip has made clear that partnerships are a vibrant and important aspect of operations in tertiary education in Australia. While partnerships may be inevitable, they are not without problematic issues. These issues, as well as the benefits of partnerships, provide valuable examples for the higher-education sectors in The Netherlands and the UK. Technology is essential for the operation of partnerships in Australia. The next two sections focus on these points.

Partnerships as a two-edged sword

With regard to partnerships for offshore course delivery, the active pursuit of external students brings many advantages to the university (and to a lesser extent, to the TAFE). Course offerings become increasingly market sensitive. Multi-cultural contacts increase. Instructors are increasingly forced to make use of new teaching techniques and technologies, simply because they must, in order to work with offshore students. This can help the process of uptake of technologies more generally into the teaching and learning process within universities. Jameson (2002) as a conclusion from a recent study in the UK, noted that 'many academics are reluctant to use technology unless pressurised to do so… However, the pressures are such that there are few institutions that will not make some provision for technology applications, because everybody else is doing so' (p. 5). Given that there are many valuable uses of technology to support learning (Technology Type 2, Figure 7), Australian universities may be moving more quickly into exploitation of the benefits of technology than Dutch and UK universities because of being pressurised by the need for external, fee-paying students.

However, there are problems with the high focus on new cohorts of fee-paying students, both on campus and offshore, in Australian universities. External students, despite screening methods, may not directly integrate into existing course offerings for reasons of background, culture and language. Extra time is required of instructors to work with the external students. On occasion, issues may arise relating to the norms that are applied to external students compared to internal students. And, although the financial benefits of external fee-paying students are clear, the cost to the instructor in terms of extra time and effort are generally not calculated.

With regard to courses for corporate clients, a strength, particularly for the TAFE sector, is strengthening the linkage between the educational institution and the workplace. The risk, however, is that curriculum and standards may be pragmatically determined, based primarily on the ideas of the paying partner rather than on the professional overview of the academic partner. Another issue with respect to company partnerships is that, if regular staff are involved, they have increasingly less time for the students in the regular programmes. The risk is present that high-visibility university staff are bought into the commercial programmes, leaving less-visible staff for on campus work.

With regard to industry partnerships in research, the benefits are similar. Money, equipment, contacts, opportunities, come in that would not be available otherwise. However, maintaining an academic perspective on the research can be difficult, as the norms and interests of the funding agency will have a large influence on the research process. The increasing reliance of universities on external funding for research also puts many faculties at risk. 'From the university perspective, earnings from external commercial relationships were found to be greatest for engineering, followed by biosciences and the physical sciences. Universities without engineering faculties appeared to have fewer opportunities for developing commercial relations' (Galagher, 2000, p. 36). In Australia, the strain on social sciences and the humanities for obtaining research funding is high in that requirements for company co-funding make it difficult if not impossible to compete for some of the major research competitions.

And even when a partnership with industry with respect to research is established, there still remain potential problems. The ability to speak, and write, critically based on research, can be curtailed. In addition to issues relating to academic freedom and ownership of intellectual property, 'Universities were reported to be finding it difficult, in developing consultancy and external earnings policies, to strike a balance between protecting themselves against legal liabilities and maintaining flexibility in their legal relations...Universities were finding that success in maximising the value of intellectual property, particularly through spin-off companies, requires

access to a critical mass of specialist professional and management resources. Larger universities were seen to be more able than smaller ones to carry the costs and risks involved' (Galagher, 2000, p. 36). The need for corporate partnerships for research funding may in fact be a mechanism leading to the demise of smaller universities not able to compete with institutions such as the University of Melbourne, not only because of the latter's depth of research capacity but also because of the latter's extensive support services for corporate-university partnerships.

In the TAFE sector, the need for industry partnerships also may serve as a constraint on the development of experience with technology support for learning within the TAFE institution itself. The use of technology in in-house industry training in Australia is still low. In 2001, it was reported that 'the number of organisations [companies] now using an intranet for learning is currently at 29%...in its infancy here compared with reports from the US...where 87% of organisations are implementing online learning at the whole company level' (OLA, 2001, p. 2-3). While the US data may be optimistic, the point remains that the need to fit in with the technology conditions and culture of the learning-training departments of companies with which the TAFE partners may hold back the general experience base with technology for teaching and learning within the TAFEs. However, it may also provide a new opportunity: the same OLA report (2001) that major reasons that industry still makes limited use of technology for training include 'lack of knowledge about online learning' and 'lack of appropriate expertise' (OLA, 2001, p. 4). For both TAFEs and universities, this represents a new partnership opportunity, assuming they have developed the expertise that is still in its infancy in the industry training sector. 'The maturation of online delivery (in the vocational education and training sector) will be realised once innovators begin to develop realistic strategic, pedagogical and commercial models' (Harper, Hedberg, Bennett, & Lockyer, 2000, p.1). Since such models are developing strongly in many Australian universities (see for example, Oliver & Herrington, 2001), the opportunity is present for Australia to make a strong move forward in applications of technology to learning in the industrial sector.

Technology and partnerships

Technology is essential for the ambitions of Australian universities with respect to increasing numbers of offshore and off campus students. Already, the realities of Australian geographic dispersion have stimulated cutting-edge research and experience with technology for flexible learning in the Australian educational-technology community (see Olivers & Herrington, 2001, and also the proceedings of the yearly ASCILITE and HERDSA www.herdsa.org.au/ conferences). Also, the need to professionally support and maintain a dispersed student body are leading to innovative technology systems for support and administration, as seen at Charles Sturt University.

In this respect, most universities in The Netherlands have yet to feel a sense of urgency or necessity with respect to technology use. The huge offshore market that Australians have discovered could also be open to Dutch higher-education institutions, if they are willing to provide instruction in English. However, with the evolution toward English-language Masters programmes that is now occurring in The Netherlands the opportunity will soon be in place for attracting an international market. Whether the motivation and sense of urgency to do so will be there is another story. In Australia, it certainly

is. If and when this sense of urgency arises, Dutch universities would be well advised to learn from the experience of Australian universities with respect to support of off campus learning with technology.

The position of UK universities in this respect appears to be intermediate between that of The Netherlands and Australia. Some have developed their technology use to levels comparable to those found in Australia, and others have ambitions to follow, but the scale of operations in the offshore market is not so great as there. The formation of 'UK eUniversities Worldwide' may be a signal that the UK is going to move closer to the Australian model.

References

Australian Vice-Chancellors' Committee (AVCC). 2002. Fact Sheet 2: The sources of university income. **www.avcc.edu.au/news/public_statements/publications/fact_sheet_2.pdf**.

Australian Vice-Chancellors' Committee (AVCC). 2002. Fact Sheet 7: University research income. **www.avcc.edu.au/news/public_statements/publications/fact_sheet_7.pdf**

Australian Vice-Chancellors' Committee (AVCC). 2001a. International links of Australian universities.**www.avcc.edu.au/policies_activities/international_relations/internationalisation_initiatives/flinks.htm**

Australian Vice-Chancellors' Committee (AVCC). 2001b. Offshore programs of Australian universities. **www.avcc.edu.au/policies_activities/international_relations/internationalisation_initiatives/offshor.htm**

Australian Vice-Chancellors' Committee (AVCC). 2000a. International relations strategic plan: 2000-2002.**www.avcc.edu.au/policies_activities/international_relations/international_relations/stratplan2000.doc**

Australian Vice-Chancellors' Committee (AVCC). 2000b. Universities forge stronger links with Indonesia. **www.avcc.edu.au/news/public_statements/speeches/2000/indonesia.htm.**

Beck, J. A, Baker, J. A., Radford, A., & & Costigan, J. 2002, March 5. The business of open learning. Paper presented at the Global Summit of Online Learning Networks, Adelaide, Australia. **www.educationau.edu.au/globalsummit/papers/jbeck.htm**

Crock, M., Joughin, G., Edwards, P., & Curtis, D. 2001. Developing strategic learning alliances: Partnerships for the provision of global education and training solutions. ALT-Journal, 9(1), 84-93.

Cunningham, S., Ryan, Y., Stedman, L., Tapsell, S., Bagdon, K., Flew, T., & Coaldrake, P. 2000. The business of borderless education. Canberra: Evaluations and Investigations Programme, Higher Education Division, DETYA

Galagher, M. 2000. The emergence of entrepreneurial public universities in Australia. Paper presented at the IMHE General Conference of the OECD, Paris. Occasional Paper Series 00/E, Department of Education, Training and Youth Affairs, Higher Education Division.

Harper, B., Hedberg, J., Bennett, S., & Lockyer, L. 2000. The online experience: The state of Australian online education and training practices. Kensington Park, SA: Australian National Training Authority.

James, R. 2002, March 20. The Australian higher education system and educational technology. Presentation to the SURF-ALT Study Trip participants, University of Melbourne, Centre for the Study of Higher Education.

Jameson, D. G. 2002. Impact of educational technology on higher education. Internal report. London: University College London. (dgordonjameson@aol.com)

OLA, 2001. The current status of online learning in Australia. Report commissioned by TAFE Frontiers and Online Learning Australia. Melbourne, Vic: TAFE Frontiers.

Oliver, R., & Herrington, J. 2001. Teaching and learning online: A beginner's guide to e-learning and e-teaching in higher education. Perth: Edith Cowan University.

Taylor, P., & Blaik, J. 2002. Project report: What have we learned? The Logan Campus 1998-2001. Brisbane: Griffith Institute for Higher Education, Griffith University.

Acronyms

ACU
  Australian Catholic University
  www.acu.edu.au/

ACUCOM
  ACU Commercial

ANTA
  Australian National Training Authority
  www.anta.gov.au/

ANU
  Australian National University
  www.anu.edu.au/

ANU-IAS
  The Institute of Advanced Studies
  www.anu.edu.au/academia/ias.html

ASCILITE
  Australasian Society for Computers In Learning In Tertiary Education
  www.ascilite.org.au/

AVCC
  Australian Vice-Chancellors' Committee
  www.avcc.edu.au/

CPA Australia
  Certified Practising Accountants
  www.cpaaustralia.com.au/

CSIRO
  Commonwealth Scientific and Industrial Research Organisation.
  www.csiro.au/

CSU
  Charles Sturt University
  www.csu.edu.au/

DET
  Dept of Education and Training

HERDSA
  Higher Education Research and Development Society of Australia
  www.herdsa.org.au/

HSC
  Higher School Certificate

IDP Australia
  International Development Program
  www.idp.com

MEI
  Melbourne Enterprises International
  www.mei.unimelb.edu.au/disclaim.htm

MUP
  Melbourne University Private
  www.muprivate.edu.au/

NCVER
  National Centre for Vocational Education Research
  www.ncver.edu.au/

NSW
  New South Wales

NUS
  National Union of Students
  www.unistudent.com.au/

OLA
  Open Learning Australia
  www.ola.edu.au/

RMIT
  Royal Melbourne Institute of Technology
  www.rmit.edu.au/

SCORM
Shareable Content Object Reference
Model initiative
www.adlnet.org/

SPIRT
Strategic Partnerships with Industry –
Research and Training
www.arc.gov.au/ncgp/old_grants/
grants_spirt.htm

TAFE
Technical and Further Education

UNSW
University of New South Wales
www.unsw.edu.au/

Appendix 1: List of participants

Jill Armstrong	Senior adviser, LTSN Generic Centre
Petra Boezerooy	Research Associate at the Centre for Higher Education and Policy Studies (CHEPS) University of Twente
Betty Collis	Professor of Tele-learning and Department Chairperson, Faculty of Educational Science and Technology, University of Twente
Bas Cordewener	Program Co-ordinator, SURF Educatief
Janet Hanson	Associate Head of Academic Services (Teaching and Learning), Bournemouth University
Robert Harding	Director Interactive Technologies in Assessment and Learning, University of Cambridge Local Examinations Syndicate (UCLES)
Martin Jenkins	Team Leader, Learning Technology and Skills Support Centre, Cheltenham & Gloucester College of Higher Education (CGCHE)
Arthur Loughran	Senior Lecturer Centre for learning and teaching (CLT), University of Paisley
Helen McEvoy	Reference and Information Assistant, Information Resources and Services John Rylands University Library of Manchester
Marcel Mirande	(at the time of the study visit: Adjunct director of the Institute for Educational and Organisational Consultance in Higher Education (IOWO), Catholic University Nijmegen. Since 1 July 2002, director of the Dutch Digital University
Wiebe Nijlunsing	Head of Product group Simulations, Business Center, Van Hall Institute
Rhonda Riachi	Director, Association for Learning Technology, Oxford Brookes University
Annette Roeters	Vice president of Windesheim, University of Professional Education in Zwolle
Martin Valcke	Professor Instructional Sciences Department of Education, Ghent University
Jan van der Veen	Co-ordinator ICT services for Education & Research, DINKEL institute, University of Twente
Barbara Watson	Learning Technologies Team Leader, University of Durham

Appendix 2: Overview of the programmes of the higher education institutions visits in Australia, March 10-22, 2002

Monday 11 - Tuesday 12 March

University of Technology Sydney

Contact person: Simon Housego Lecturer, Institute for Interactive Media & Learning

Day 1

- 10:00 SA meets with SURF/ALT-C team Level 27 The UTS Experience with ICT

- 10:30 IML Roundtable - IML New Media Lab, Level 27

- 11:00 Morning tea followed by open discussion with SURF/ALT-C group

- 12:30 Lunch

- 14:00 FLAG Meeting

- 16:00 Finish

Day 2

Faculty of Education, Haymarket Campus

Contact person: Dr Sandy Schuck Senior Lecturer, Faculty of Education

- Morning: visit Faculty of Education

- Afternoon: Kuri-gai campus, Lindfield

University of Wollongong

Contact person: Gerry Lefoe Lecturer, Educational Development Services, CEDIR

Day 1

- 10:00 Welcome by Rob Castle, Pro Vice-Chancellor Academic UoW

- 10:15 Overview of E-learning at UoW and CEDIR Tour ; Sandra Wills, Director CEDIR, Gerry Lefoe, Educational Development Services, CEDIR, Russ Pennell, Flexible Learning Services, CEDIR, Helen Carter, Manager Flexible Learning Services, CEDIR

- 11:00 Morning tea

- 11:30 South Coast Project-Arts, Rebecca Albury, Assistant Dean Faculty of Arts, Craig Littler, Library – Remote Services Manager (services to off campus students), Neil Trivett, Lecturer Learning Development (student support), Kate Bowles, Subject Developer & online teacher, Gerry Lefoe, Educational Development Services, CEDIR, Cath Ellis, Subject Coordinator

- 12:00 Lunch

- 13:30 Learning Online Team, Russ Pennell, Flexible Learning Services, CEDIR, Gloria Wood, Victor Ossington, Gerry Lefoe, Educational Development Services, CEDIR, Craig Littler, Library

- 14:30 Phototonics Outreach program: Innovative IT and science training on broadband networks

- 15:00 Faculty Service Agreement (Project Management Database), Helen Carter, Manager Flexible Learning Services, CEDIR, Sarah Lambert, Flexible Learning Services, CEDIR Bob Corderoy, Educational Development Services, CEDIR

- 15:45 Library: e-learning initiatives Lynne Wright

- 16:30 Finish

Day 2

- 09:30 Welcome and tour of emlab/resources John Hedberg, director of RILE & emlab Brian Ferry, Deputy director of RILE

- 10:15 AUTC Project - Use of ICTS in Flexible Delivery, Lori Lockyer, member of RILE, Faculty of Education. John G. Hedberg, director of RILE and emlab, Faculty of Education. Shirley Agostinho, member of RILE.

- 10.45 Morning Tea RILE members

- 11.15 Online teaching in SE Asia, Research in Interactive learning Environments Christine Brown, member of RILE, Faculty of Education.

- 12.00 Lunch

- afternoon: visit own contacts or join at meeting with the CERG group

Charles Sturt University

Contact person: Dr John Messing Sub-dean, Teaching Quality, Faculty of Science & Agriculture Director, Research Centre for Innovation in Telelearning Environments

Day 1
- 10:30 Welcome Morning Tea School of Information Studies

- 11:00 Overview of CSU online operations, Dr. John Messing - Sub-Dean, Teaching Quality, Faculty of Science & Agriculture , Director, Research Centre for Innovation in Telelearning Environments, School of Information Studies.

- 12:30 Lunch

- 13:30 Meetings with Directors/associate directors of Centre for Enhancing Learning Teaching, Petrina Quinn, Milena Dunn, Roger Murphy, Jill Harris

- 15:00 Afternoon tea break

- 15:30 Meetings with manager of CSU Online & Div of Information Technology – Les Burr

- 19:00 Dinner

Day 2
- 9:00 Meetings/demonstrations from CELT/Learning Materials Centre

- 10:30 Morning tea

- 11:00 Individual presentations by teachers to each of the 5 group members on some aspects eg. 3D Virtual Chemistry, Moos, integration with administration systems use of forums, online assignment submission etc

- 12:30 lunch with staff members

- 13:30 Final wrap-up session at your discretion

- 15:00 Afternoon tea

- 15.30 Return to Sydney

Wednesday 13 March

Zing Conference Systems, John Findlay:

- Tour Technology Park

- First evaluation session

Thursday 14 March

Edith Cowan University

Contact person: Prof Ron Oliver Director of the Centre for Research in Information Technology and Communications

- 09:00 Meeting with Ron Oliver and members of the centre; Jen Harrington, Joe Luca Chris Brooke and Mark McMahon.

- 10:00 Morning tea with Head of School and Dean of faculty and other members.

- 10:30 Meeting with Head of Resources Development Centre at ECU and development staff.

- 12:00 Meeting with Deputy Vice-Chancellor, Pro Vice-Chancellor International and Director of the Learning Innovations and Future Developments Centre; Dr. Ann Deden and Jackie Willis, Head of Resources Development Centre at ECU.

- 12:30 Lunch.

- 14:00 Meeting with Head of Professional Development Centre and other staff.

- 15:30 Afternoon tea and disburse.

Thursday 14 – Friday 15 March

Southern Cross University

Contact person: Meg O'Reilly Educational Designer Teaching & Learning Centre

Day 1

- 09:00 Welcome by TLC
  Introductions from sections of TLC and overview of flexible learning: Institutional level, technical implementation and teaching and learning level.

- 10:30 Coffee

- 11:00 Introductions to Southern Cross OnLine (SCOL)

- 12:00 Introductions to senior management

- 12:40 lunch

- 13.40 Library
  Introductions from library, overview of network services and copyright: Institutional level, technical implementation and reference to teaching and learning collaborations.

- 14:40 Coffee

- 15:00 Staff seminar by visitors, hosted by TLC

- 17:00 Finish

Day 2

- 09:00 Meeting academic staff

- 11:00 Coffee

- 11:30 Meeting academic staff

- 13:30 Lunch

- 14:30 Onwards – consultation time

Queensland University of Technology

Contact person: Helmut Geiblinger, PhD Assistant Manager SMILE, TALSS, QUT

Day 1

- 09:00 Meeting Mr Neil Thelander, Director Rotation ITS/TALSS, Relationship b/w ITS, library, TALSS
- 10:30 Morning tea
- 10:45 Meeting Mr Tom Cochrane, QUT Strategy Institutional vision
- 11:30 Meeting Prof Gail Hart, Impact of Teaching and Learning
- 12:30 Lunch
- 14:00 Meeting Ms Halima Goss, Communities of practice Partnerships with faculties
- 16:00 Finish

Day 2

- 09:00 Meeting Prof Peter Coaldrake, Corporate Universities' Business of Borderless Education Project
- 10:00 Meeting Mr Michael Ryan, Faculty approach to online teaching
- afternoon: visit own contacts

Friday 15 March

Murdoch University

Contact person: Dr Rob Philips Senior Lecturer Teaching and Learning Centre

- 09:00 Arrive and settle in

- 09:30 Effects of the use of ICT on learning and teaching, CUTSD evaluation project

- 11:30 Institutional changes, changes in structure of teaching

- 12:30 Lunch

- 14:00 Managing and implementing electronic learning environments.
  Murdoch online mainstreaming project

- 15:00 Pedagogy of online learning, discussion of educational design and staff development
  approaches, demonstration

- 16:30 Developing and implementation of ICT. Factor affecting adoption, proj. management.

- 17:00 Finish

Monday 18 March

University of Western Australia

Contact person: Dr Jan Dook, Faculty of Science CATLyst, WebCT Co-ordinator Centre for
Learning Technology

- 09.00 Welcome from Alan Robson, Deputy Vice-Chancellor and CATL overview
  Deborah Ingram, Co-ordinator Centre for the Advancement of Teaching and Learning
  (Organisational and Staff Development Services)

- 09.30 Example of Innovative Teaching and Learning, Nathan Scott, Lecturer Department of
  Mechanical and Materials Engineering/Mechanical & Materials Engineering (Faculty of
  Engineering, Computing and Mathematics)

- 10.15 Morning Tea

- 10.45 Example of Innovative Teaching and Learning, Mike Fardon, Faculty of Arts Multimedia Centre
  (Faculty of Arts, Humanities and Social Sciences), David Coall and Jassie Tunstill, School of
  Anatomy and Human Biology, Eileen Thompson and other staff.

- 11.30 ALT-Surf presentation

155

WestOne

Contact person: Stuart Young Director Products & Technology

- 13:30 Introductions, Stuart Young, Director Products & Technology, and Sue Lapham, Director of Corporate Development

- 13:45 Site inspection

- 14:00 Presentations and questions:

  - Australian Vocational Education & Training System

  - Flexible Learning Framework

  - Online Learning Delivery

  - Publications

  - Discussion

- 17:00 Closing

Griffith University

Contact person: Lynda Davies Personal Assistant to Director

- 09:00 Meeting GIHE staff

- 10:00 Meeting Phil Rowan, Campus Co-ordinator

- 11:00 Meeting Cheryl Brown, Flexible Learning Access Services

- 12:00 Lunch, incl. drive to Nathan Campus

- 14:00 Meeting Janice Rickards, Pro-Vice-Chancellor

- 14:45 Travel to Mt Gravatt Campus

- 15:00 Meeting Linda Conrad, Acting Director Griffith Institute. for Higher Education

- 15:30 Afternoon tea and discussion with GIHE academics

- 16:00 Conclusion of visit and closing

University of Southern Queensland

Contact person: Susan Brosnan Executive Assistant to Director, Distance Education centre

- 10:30 Welcome to USQ: Professor Jim Taylor (Deputy Vice-Chancellor – Global Learning Services),
  Mrs Jannette Kirkwood (Head, Design & Development),
  Mrs Judy Timmins, (Head, Operations and Management Services).

- 10:50 DEC overview and online demo: Professor Jim Taylor (Deputy Vice-Chancellor –
  Global Learning Services).

- 11:30 Tour of the DEC: Mrs Jannette Kirkwood (Head, Design & Development).

- 12:15 Discussion online, teaching and learning; Associate Professor Glen Postle
  (Distance Education Centre/Faculty of Education).

- 13:00 Lunch

- 14:00 ICT at the strategic level: Dr Jeff Mcdonell (Director, Information Technology Services).

- 15:00 Library services and information recourses tour of library; Ms Madeleine Mcpherson
  (University Librarian).

- 15:00 An Alternative assessment/evaluation: Associate Professor Andrew Sturman
  (Faculty of Education).

- 16:00 Closing

Wednesday 20 March

- 9.30-12.00 2nd evaluation session

Wednesday 20 – Thursday 21 March

University of Melbourne

Contact person: Christine Mason Personal Assistant to the Director, Teaching, Learning and Research Support Department

Day 1

- 14:00 Meeting Richard James, Peter Harris and Som Naidu: discussions

- 17:00 Social activity, open meeting

- 17:30 Closing

Day 2

- 09:00 Meeting Julie Rodman, U21 Collaboration initiatives intellectual property

- 10:00 Morning tea

- 10:30 Visit Percy Baxter Collaborative Learning Centre: technical infrastructure, support services, E-learning strategies, learning management systems, Susan Bray, Patrick Blanchard and Karen Kealy

- 12:30 Lunchtime seminar: presentation by visitors

- 14:00 Teaching and learning level: representatives of the Multimedia Co-ordination Group

- 15:00 Afternoon tea and meeting Susan Bray on Learning Resources Catalogue

- 16:00 Meeting Som Naidu and Paul Fritze on Impact of ICT on teaching and learning

- 17:00 Closing

Monash University

Contact person: Anthony Gilding Centre for Learning and Teaching Support

Day 1

- Afternoon meeting with several staff members:

- 14:00 Discussion on current developments and future directions for Electronically Supported Teaching and Learning at Monash University

- 15:00 Discussion on use of ICT in teaching and learning

- 16:00 Discussion on Quality in HE

- 17:00 Closing

Day 2

- 10:00 Discussion on Central Learning management systems: the WebCT project

- 11:00 Free time

- 12:30 Lunch meeting: European developments in the use of ICT to support teaching and learning

- 14:00 Discussion on academic Support Network for use of ICT in Teaching and Learning

- 15:00 Faculty perspective: use of ICT in teaching and learning, support and quality

- 16:00 Professional development

- 17:00 Closing

Deakin University

Contact person: Rod Sims Learning Environments

Day 1
Burwood Campus, Melbourne

- Morning: drive to Burwood Campus

- 13:00 Welcome

- 13:30 Deakin Online, Brian Corbitt, Jocelyn Calvert, Rod Sims

- 14:30 Afternoon tea

- 15:00 Faculty of Arts Initiatives, Joan Beamont, Viola Rosario

- 16:00 Faculty of Health & Behavioural Sciences, Ian Story

Day 2
Waterfront Campus, Geelong

- 08:00 Drive to Geelong

- 09:30 Faculty of Education Initiatives, Shirley Grundy, Terry Evans, Elizabeth Stacey, Colin Warren

- 10:30 Faculty of Business & Law Initiatives, Ray Bantow, Christine Goodwin

- 11:30 Faculty of Science & Technology Initiatives, Jo Caldwell

- 12:30 Lunch

- 14:00 Learning Services, Sue McKnight, Rod Sims
  Learning Management Systems, Ian Smissen
  Educational Research, Di Challis
  Educational Innovation, Stephen Segrave, Glenn McNolty

- 16:00 Visit Wrap-up

Friday 22 March, all participants

Visit to DEST in Melbourne

- Third evaluation session